MAKING the NUMBERS COUNT

Second Edition

The Accountant as Change Agent on the World Class Team

MAKING the NUMBERS COUNT

Second Edition

The Accountant as Change Agent
on the World Class Team

BRIAN H. MASKELL

CRC Press
Taylor & Francis Group
Boca Raton   London   New York

CRC Press is an imprint of the
Taylor & Francis Group, an **informa** business

A PRODUCTIVITY PRESS BOOK

Productivity Press
Taylor & Francis Group
270 Madison Avenue
New York, NY 10016

© 2009 by Taylor and Francis Group, LLC
Productivity Press is an imprint of Taylor & Francis Group, an Informa business

No claim to original U.S. Government works

Printed in the United States of America on acid-free paper
10 9 8 7 6 5 4 3 2 1

International Standard Book Number: 978-1-4200-9060-4 (Hardback)

Library of Congress Cataloging-in-Publication Data

Maskell, Brian H.
    Making the numbers count : the accountant as change agent on the world-class team / Brian H. Maskell. -- 2nd ed.
        p. cm.
    Includes bibliographical references and index.
    ISBN 978-1-4200-9060-4 (hardcover : alk. paper)
    1. Managerial accounting. 2. Accountants. 3. Industrial management. I. Title.

HF5657.4.M375 2009
658.15'11--dc22   2009013222

Visit the Taylor & Francis Web site at
http://www.taylorandfrancis.com

and the Productivity Press Web site at
http://www.productivitypress.com

Contents

Preface to the First Edition

Working as I have with many manufacturing companies striving to achieve excellence, it has become apparent to me that accountants play a crucial role in any company. Sadly, in most companies, accountants are a part of the problem and rarely a part of the solution. We speak much in the lean manufacturing movement about the elimination of waste in the processes; but the biggest waste I see is the waste of human talent, energy, and creativity throughout Western industry. Accountants are primarily bookkeepers and offer very little more to their companies; this is a tragic waste.

This book is not intended to provide a detailed explanation of new accounting methods; there are many other books that do so.* Instead, it is intended to be a call to arms for accountants who want to stop "wasting" their time and begin to make an important contribution to their companies. All accounting tasks are non-value-added, but accountants can become highly value-added to their organizations if they can come out from under the ledgers and focus on change and improvement.

The working title for this book over the last two years had been *The Accountant as an Agent of Change*. Many of my colleagues were amused by this title, and they made wisecracks about the traditional idea of accountants as dull and conservative people who would not recognize an innovation if they stumbled over it, let alone be able to initiate new thinking and change. Yet this is exactly the role accountants must actively seek if they are to be relevant to a company making the transition to a lean enterprise.

Of all the business issues we face, accounting functions are the ones that can be most readily automated. The bookkeeping and primary report presentations are all regulated by law or by accepted practice, and all business software systems provide the ability to significantly automate these tasks. The accountant's first responsibility is to significantly reduce the amount of time and effort required to do the routine bookkeeping and reporting

---

* *Practical Lean Accounting*, by Brian H. Maskell and Bruce L. Baggaley, Productivity Press, New York, 2003. *The Lean Business Management System*, by Brian Maskell and the BMA Team, edited by Susan J. Lilly, BMA Press, Cherry Hill, NJ, 2007.

by eliminating much of the traditional accounting system as the company moves into lean and gains greater control of its processes. He or she can also see to it that computer systems are used intelligently to eliminate the basic "grunt" work of posting transactions, handling payables and receivables, presenting the monthly books, and so forth.

Once his or her time is freed from the chains of the ledger and the computer screen, the accountant can begin the process of becoming a change agent. This is done by gaining a detailed and comprehensive understanding of the business, the products, the marketplace, and the myriad other activities of a modern manufacturing company. The job is then to work with others throughout the company to create change and improvement. Accountants must challenge themselves to come out of the cozy back room and become street fighters for change—to work with other people in the company to create customer value; eliminate waste; improve processes; create partnerships with customers, suppliers, and other third parties; and develop a truly lean organization that is capable of taking advantage of the turbulent and unpredictable times in which we work.

No book is a solo effort. The ideas and concepts presented throughout this book have been drawn from many sources and inspired by many people. I am indebted to my friends and colleagues at BMA Inc. and BMA Europe Ltd., including Bruce Baggaley, Nick Katko, Susan Lilly, David Paino, and Ross Maynard, who have contributed a great deal to the ideas within this book and have been excellent sparring partners. I am grateful for the help and kindness I have received from Orry Fiume, Jerry Solomon, Robin Cooper, Fred Garbinski, and Jim Huntzinger and his Lean Accounting Summit team. I am also indebted to the many clients I have worked with over the years—too many to mention by name—who have striven to make excellence a reality in their organizations. It is easy and inspiring to create a vision for where a company should be going, but it is only the hard work, dedication, and excellence shown by the people within the company that can turn the vision into reality. It has been my privilege to work with many such people over the last couple of decades.

These are challenging times for manufacturers, distributors, service companies, and every organization that is faced with the new competition of the global marketplace. This book is intended to inspire accountants within these companies to make a big contribution and help their companies become winners. If you would like to discuss these issues further, please feel free to contact me.

Brian H. Maskell

BMA Inc., Cherry Hill, NJ

bmaskell@maskell.com

+1 609 239 1080

www.maskell.com

Preface to the Second Edition

Since it was first published in 1996, *Making the Numbers Count* has been very successful. When I first wrote the book, I wanted to throw down a gauntlet to the finance and accounting people in Western manufacturing companies. The book is a polemic. It makes the case for a change of role for financial controllers, and it indicates new directions for both management and financial accounting.

In what way has the book been successful? Did it hit the best-sellers list? No. Did the author rake in millions on book royalties? No. Instead, *Making the Numbers Count* raised the right questions, had an impact on a lot of people, and has been instrumental in helping to create the "lean accounting movement."

There was very little understanding or acceptance of lean accounting in 1996. People attending public training classes were often challenging and hostile. But the tide turned about the year 2002. The attitude of people attending training seminars changed to "show us how to make these changes." Since then, hundreds of companies have taken the road of lean accounting. Some of those companies are huge multinational corporations, and others are smaller, privately held organizations that are the bedrock of American industry.

There are many reason for these changes. The publication of *Lean Thinking* by Jones and Womack (1996) brought lean to the forefront. There are a lot of vigorous pioneer organizations showing that lean really works. These—together with conferences, journal publications, and other events—raised the profile of lean manufacturing and lean accounting. I believe that *Making the Numbers Count* played a role in this transition. We met our objective. I have received many phone calls and e-mails from finance people in fledgling lean organizations. Some read the book and forged ahead with their own lean accounting ideas. Others worked with us to help make these changes in their companies. Others went on to become vocal advocates. Academe became intrigued with lean accounting. Over the last few years, it seems like every time I turn around, there is a professor asking questions about lean accounting. For the last five years, there has been a lean accounting summit conference focused on exploring the practicalities of lean accounting. The organizers of the summit conference were the ones who started to use the term "lean accounting movement."

So why did Productivity Press decide to publish a second edition of *Making the Numbers Count*? The book went out of print in 2004 when our newer book, *Practical Lean Accounting,* was published. I felt that *Making the Numbers Count* had served its time and that the detailed and more systematic approach of the new book was what the market required. Well, I was wrong. Initially, we got complaints from people wanting to buy the book and not finding it available. Then we learned that some of the professors found this book to be a more accessible text for their students. One professor had her students photocopy the entire book because they could not buy it at the book store. Then we found that used copies of the book were selling on eBay—sometimes for ten times the face price! Therefore, we decided to publish a second edition because there is clearly demand for a book like *Making the Numbers Count.*

Owing to the acceptance of the original book, I have tried to take a light touch in updating the second edition. Most of the changes have been in the details and the terminology. I have also tried to maintain the easy-to-read style of the first edition, and to keep up the humor and irreverence of the original. The word *lean* did not appear in the first edition, but I have peppered it around this new edition. I have corrected some of the errors and updated some of the ideas. The only chapter that has been completely rewritten is Chapter 5 on the new cost-accounting methods. In the first edition, this chapter dealt with activity-based costing and management (ABC/M). We discovered by about 1998 that ABC/M has no place in lean accounting and that ABC/M is equally as troublesome as standard costing for lean organizations, perhaps even more so owing to its complexity. Therefore, Chapter 5 now addresses value-stream accounting. Value-stream accounting methods have been tried and tested in many diverse companies over the last 10 years, sometimes with our help, and other times independently. Such methods have proved to be very useful and very lean. They focus on customer value; they work by value stream; they address and enhance process flow; they empower people; and they motivate continuous improvement and the pursuit of perfection.

The first edition of the book succeeded by helping to raise the profile of lean accounting and to challenge accountants and controllers in Western manufacturing companies to rethink their roles and their methods in the light of lean transformation. I hope that as you read this new edition, you will also be challenged and inspired to eliminate the waste in your own processes and become an agent of change.

Brian H. Maskell
BMA Inc., Cherry Hill, NJ
bmaskell@maskell.com
+1 609 239 1080
www.maskell.com

1

The Proactive Accountant

Management accounting is a profession under fire. In the last few years a barrage of criticism has been leveled at the traditional techniques of management accounting, as well as at management accountants and financial controllers. The fusillade has come from the accounting press, other trade and academic journals, and from people within manufacturing organizations. The author recently conducted a (very informal) survey in several American manufacturing companies.

The results were decidedly unflattering. It appears that management accountants are generally held in low regard by their colleagues and are not considered to be playing a useful role. The information they present is seen as wasteful, misleading, and causing more problems than it solves. Why is this?

The survey asked the following questions:

- What word *best* describes the management accountants in your company?
- What word *least* describes the management accountants in your company?

innovative	*proactive*	*valuable*	*boring*
tricky	*progressive*	*isolated*	*dishonest*
unhelpful	*irrelevant*	*in touch*	*team member*

The survey results were: The words that *best* describe management accountants are *boring, unhelpful, isolated*. The words that *least* describe management accountants are *innovative, proactive, progressive*.

It used to be that companies were "run by the numbers"—many still are—that came from the accounting department. It was generally accepted that managers needed this information to keep a finger on the pulse of the organization, to improve productivity, reduce inventory, and increase profitability. The monthly variance reports and budget analysis were the primary mechanisms for understanding the company's effectiveness. Capital investment projects lived or died based on the accounting analysis of return on investment (ROI) and discounted cash flow (DCF). What are the reasons for this fall from grace?

MANUFACTURING IN THE TWENTY-FIRST CENTURY

The world of manufacturing has changed beyond recognition in the last 30 years. Foreign competitors attacked Western markets in the late 1970s and decimated whole industries. They stole our markets by being better. American and European manufacturers recognized that they had to change, change fast, and change radically.

In the early 1980s, quality became the issue. The better Japanese manufacturers could make products of significantly higher quality than we could. Western companies began to learn their "secrets": statistical process control to reduce variation, quality at source instead of inspection, PDCA (plan, do, check, act) problem solving, design for manufacture, and certified suppliers delivering on time with zero defects. The quality revolution hit hard. There are no quick fixes to create quality overnight. It takes long-term commitment and an attention to detail that are foreign to most organizations. (Quality, lean manufacturing, and other world-class methods are discussed in more detail in Chapter 3.)

The new competitors were also more nimble. They could introduce new products faster, were more responsive to the customer's needs, and had shorter lead times and much lower costs. In response, Western manufacturers began to introduce lean manufacturing techniques: short cycle times, small batches, changeovers of less than 10 minutes, cellular manufacturing, synchronized production flow, kanban, and low, low inventories. These approaches broke all the rules.

The need to slim down overheads led to cataclysmic organizational changes. Autocracy and bureaucracy were replaced by the team approach and employee involvement. Responsibility was shifted to the sharp end of the business: the shop floor, the warehouse, the design team, and the office. A work environment was created where all employees were responsible for their own quality, their own schedules, continuous improvement, and creating customer value.

Parallel with these changes was an increasing understanding that traditional costing methods were no longer relevant. The patterns of product costs had changed over the years as technology, production methods, and the market had changed. Studies showed that the standard product costs generated by the cost accountants were misleading and wrong. There were fundamental flaws in the tried-and-true accounting practices. (The problems caused by traditional accounting methods are discussed more fully in Chapter 2.)

What was happening to the accounting department during this maelstrom of change? Nothing. The same systems, the same methods, the same approaches. The real issues of manufacturing became quality, on-time delivery, continuous improvement, customer value, time to market, and employee involvement. The accounting departments largely ignored these issues.

CRITICISM OF ACCOUNTANTS AND CONTROLLERS

A company moving into a teamwork approach cannot have a parochial and isolated accounting group. Everybody else in the organization is getting cross-trained, is committed to quality and continuous improvement, and is on a team—or several teams. The barriers must be broken down and the departmental silos eliminated; the entire organization must work together to achieve common objectives. The accountants—along with the industrial engineers, the designers, the quality people, the maintenance staff, and other support groups—must become part of the team.

The introduction of lean manufacturing requires the elimination of complex and wasteful systems. Some of the most complex and wasteful systems in many companies are in accounting; these include

Budgeting
Inventory valuation

Labor reporting
Accounts payables
The entire cost-accounting system

Many of the traditional accounting methods are not only wasteful, but positively harmful to the organization. Accountants must become proactive about simplification. This requires the elimination of most of the systems that are near and dear to us, that have been our bread and butter since we left college. (Chapter 4 provides a step-by-step approach to simplifying accounting systems.)

The accounting department is frequently accused of holding back progress to lean enterprise. This is sometimes true. Accountants tend to be conservative. Our training has given us a bias toward an arms-length approach to others in the organization. Our adherence to "generally accepted accounting practice" (GAAP) has led to a lack of imagination and innovation. We must reverse this and become innovative leaders in our companies, applying our analytical skills and financial savvy to creating a world-class company. This will require a significant change of role for the accountant. But it opens up important new opportunities. These opportunities require learning new skills, working in teams, and even folding the management accounting department into the company's value-streams. These changes are not easy to make, but they are essential.

THE PROACTIVE ACCOUNTANT

The author has observed that the attitude of accountants in companies implementing lean manufacturing varies considerably from one organization to the next. In some companies accountants are "on the team," and are leaders in the quest for change and perfection. In other companies the accountants actively oppose change. The people who are bent on innovation and improvement must fight the accountants either by working around them or by the fine art of Machiavellian politicking. In most companies the accountants "do their own thing" despite the revolution taking place around their ears.

If you accept the assertion that all companies must improve radically if they are to remain competitive in our "white-knuckle times," then you must recognize that radical change is needed in the accounting department. The accountant must become proactive. He or she must become a leader for change and accept the change of role this requires.

This challenge is not unique to accountants. Radical change is taking place in all departments of the company. The introduction of lean manufacturing on the shop floor is changing the lives of managers, operators, and supervisors alike. Lean design and concurrent engineering are making the jobs of the design engineer, industrial engineer, and quality worker totally different. The trend toward a value-focused organization is changing the role of marketing, sales, and customer support personnel. Everyone's job is changing dramatically; accountants are not exempt.

In recent years the move toward lean manufacturing has been driven primarily by operations managers, quality assurance staff, and lean specialists. The accountants and other support staff have tended to stand by and watch—or hold back progress. This is no longer the case. In many world-class companies the accountants are becoming proactive leaders, creating excellence not only in their own areas of responsibility, but also across entire companies.

ATTRIBUTES OF A WORLD-CLASS MANAGEMENT ACCOUNTANT

Flexibility is an underlying theme of lean manufacturing. The management accountant must become flexible in his or her approach. First, the accountant must become a team player. There is no room for the old isolation of the accounting office. The accountant will find himself or herself on the value-stream team, on the shop floor working with the operators and supervisors, in the design office working on concurrent engineering, or working with marketing on customer service issues. These groups will often be empowered value-stream teams making constant change and improvement; the accountant must be one of the team.

Coupled with the change to teamwork is an enthusiasm for diverse activities. New vistas of opportunity and challenge are open to proactive accountants. The old cost-accounting days are now long gone. The accountant is participating in the full gamut of business activities: new product planning, marketing, customer service, production, quality, continuous improvement, as well as financially driven projects.

A keystone of lean enterprise is a bias toward simplicity. Accountants, and Western industry in general, have in the past had a proclivity to complexity. The operations-research mentality used to prevail: if you have a complex problem, find a complex method of analyzing and solving the problem. Lean manufacturers take the opposite view. If you have a complex problem, simplify it. It is easy to invent complicated solutions, but it requires skill and ingenuity to simplify a problem. Accountants need to recognize that their role is to simplify problems and eliminate complex systems, including the accounting systems.

An important aspect of simplicity is a willingness to abandon traditional approaches. The spurious argument given time and again by reluctant accountants is that they must adhere to GAAP. This is true of financial accounting because the government has a bad habit of putting financial accountants in jail if they violate accounting practice.* But the internal control of an organization is entirely under the control of the company itself. The accounting methods used must support the company's lean objectives. This means that the accounting systems must become the servants of production, sales, marketing, and engineering—not the other way round.

These kinds of changes cannot be made in a vacuum. Another attribute of a proactive accountant is a willingness to learn. So much is changing in modern business. Some of these changes are technical, some of them—the more far-reaching ones—are philosophical. It is important to be a learner.

What has been discussed in the preceding paragraphs is a revolution in thinking and practice for the average accountant.† We need to take these revolutionary steps if our companies are to be competitive in the global market of the twenty-first century.

---

* If you take a close look at GAAP, IAS (International Accounting Standards), or the Sarbanes–Oxley Act of 2002, you find that the requirements are largely sensible and straightforward. The complexity comes from a company's approach to adherence to the standards. There are many examples of organizations with very lean accounting processes that are fully compliant with these standards.

† One of my colleagues stated that he had to "rewire his brain" when coming to grips with lean accounting.

TOOLS AND TECHNIQUES

As we move our analytical skills into new areas of the production organization and abandon many of the traditional methods, there are new techniques we must learn. The first approach is very general. The average accountant is woefully ignorant of the company's processes and procedures. Many do not have a clear understanding of the accounting and administration procedures because these tend to be complex and convoluted. Very few have more than a passing knowledge of the manufacturing processes, not to mention the engineering and technology the product uses. To be a valuable contributor to your organization you must be intimately familiar with the company's products, processes, markets, and customers. You must also have a clear understanding of what people in other departments think, feel, and do. These things are not learned in training classes. They are learned by taking the time and effort—often in your own time—to get alongside other people in your organization and become a part of the team.

In addition, there are many tools and techniques that can be learned in the classroom. The following list is not exhaustive. It is intended to show the diversity of activities a world-class management accountant can participate in. In later chapters we will look at these methods in more detail.

- *Value-stream costing*: Lean organizations do not track product costs or the costs of a work order. They have simple methods to report the direct costs of the value-streams, with little or no cost allocation.
- *Value-stream management*: Lean organizations work by value-streams, and the management of the business is based around the control and improvement of the value-stream processes. Financial decisions are made with reference to the impact on the costs and profitability of the value-streams.
- *Customer value*: The starting point of lean thinking is to make the value created for the customer the primary focus of the business. The obsession with stock price (value to the owners), common among American public companies, is foreign to the lean organization.
- *Performance measurement*: Lean organizations abandon traditional financial performance measures and instead develop performance measures that are congruent with the company's lean transformation.

- *Value-added analysis*: Lean accountants understand the company's sales, marketing, design, production, distribution, support, and administrative processes with a view to identifying what adds value and what does not. This is a powerful tool for understanding and improvement.
- *Value-stream and process mapping*: Lean accountants use this graphical, team-based method of analyzing a process to create improvement.
- *Target costing*: This is a technique for matching planned product costs with customer value of the product during all phases of the product's life cycle.
- *Value engineering*: This is a formal process for driving business improvement directly from a profound understanding of how value is created for the customer.
- *Variety effectiveness process*: This is a systematic approach to reducing cost and complexity through standardization of components and production processes while providing customers with a wide choice.
- *Life-cycle costing*: This is an analysis of product costs and profitability across the entire life of the product or product family; it is a long-term view from the company's perspective and that of the customer.
- *Evaluating the financial impact of lean change and improvement*: Lean improvement cannot be understood using the cost-savings studies beloved by traditional organizations. Value-stream box scores provide insight into the true impact of lean changes.
- *Product costing*: Lean companies do not use product costs because there is no satisfactory method for calculating them. Most routine decisions are made using the value-stream box score and by assessing the impact of the decision on the value-stream as a whole, not the individual product cost. If a product cost is required, there are simple calculation methods, but product cost should not be used for any important function.

THE ROLE OF THE MANAGEMENT ACCOUNTANT

The role of the management accountant changes radically in a world-class manufacturing environment. The accountant becomes useful. This is a paradigm change. Management accounting in traditional organizations constitutes a non-value-added overhead. The accountant gathers data, creates reports, uncovers variances, analyzes projects, and creates budgets. None of these activities creates improvement; indeed, the process is wasteful, confusing, and impedes the progress of a company striving to become a world-class competitor.

Toshiro Hiromoto, the Japanese pundit, wrote, "One of the areas I believe contributes mightily to Japanese competitiveness is how many companies' management accounting systems reinforce top-to-bottom commitment to process and product innovation" (Hiromoto 1988). Many studies of Japanese management accounting methods have concluded that lean Japanese companies use management accounting methods similar to those of Western companies. Nothing could be further from the truth. They are so different that Western "experts" cannot recognize the differences. The fundamental role of accountants in the better Japanese companies is to create improvement and cost reduction, very often during the product design process at the source of cost. Many of the accounting methods are similar to those of the West; however, the concepts of accounting are fundamentally different.

The new role for management accountants is to line themselves up with the lean goals of the organization, become part of the value-stream team, and help the company move ahead. This requires flexibility, a willingness to change, and a desire to become involved in the real issues facing the organization. This new role can be uncomfortable, but it is also challenging and rewarding.

These are some of the activities in which an accountant will participate as part of the value-stream team:

- Manufacturing:
  Actively participate in lean improvement tasks, including kaizen events, continuous improvement projects, and "just-do-it" changes
  Participate in the value-stream's daily, weekly, and monthly meetings and gemba walks as a part of the value-stream team
  Assess the future impact of value-stream improvement and how the company can benefit from these changes
  Assist the value-stream team to use the performance measurements boards (cell, department, and value-stream) to control and improve the processes
  Create and use value-stream box scores for decision-making activities

- Purchasing

  Implement programs related to supplier reduction, long-term supplier relationships, supplier certification, and target costing of purchased items and materials

  Use value-stream cost information to assist with sourcing decisions, particularly make or buy decisions

- Product development:

  Be part of a concurrent-engineering team using target costing, value engineering, life-cycle costing, and other world-class methods

  Provide cost and performance information for the product-development value-stream team to bring control and improvement to their processes

- Sales and marketing:

  Support value-based sales and marketing, introduce methods for value based pricing, assess quoting opportunities using value-stream box scores, apply target costing to customer service activities, work to eliminate sales and marketing policies that are counter to lean (quantity discounts, for example)

  Implement value-based pricing; target costing of customer service activities as well as customer and product profitability

- Waste elimination:

  Become familiar with value-added analysis, value-stream management, lead-time reduction, and continuous improvement

  Radically eliminate waste from the company's accounting processes

- Performance measurement:

  Develop nonfinancial, focused performance-measurement systems in line with the company's strategic direction

- Accounting simplification:

  Systematically eliminate complex and wasteful accounting, product costing, variance reporting, budgeting, inventory control procedures, purchasing, accounts payable, receivables, and financial reporting

- Human resources:

  Establish simple, motivational profit-sharing processes so that everyone participates in the company's success

SUMMARY

Most of what a traditional management accountant does is irrelevant, wasteful, and potentially harmful to a lean company. There is a vital new role for accountants who are prepared to become proactive contributors to a company's world-class goals.

A lean accountant must be:

- Flexible
- A team member
- Willing to participate in diverse improvement activities
- Biased toward simplicity
- Willing to abandon traditional methods
- Aware of the need for education and training

QUESTIONS

1. Why are traditional management accountants regarded as irrelevant and wasteful by world-class manufacturing people?
2. How can the management accountant become a proactive part of the world-class team?
3. What are the attributes of a world-class management accountant?
4. What are some of the techniques a management accountant should add to his or her toolbox?
5. What kinds of projects and teams can benefit from the participation of a proactive management accountant?

2

*Shortcomings of Traditional Accounting Methods**

Professors Kaplan and Johnson, authors of the influential book *Relevance Lost: The Rise and Fall of Management Accounting,* have stated that cost accounting is the number one enemy of productivity (Kaplan and Johnson 1987). Strong words. There are three principal shortcomings of traditional accounting systems:

1. They are irrelevant and harmful to a business.
2. They are expensive to maintain.
3. They divert the accountant's attention from more important matters.

The average accountant in an American manufacturing company spends up to 75% of his or her time on bookkeeping activities and less than 10% on analysis and process improvement. The job has been reduced to a backward-looking, reactive recording and dissemination of data that, if it could be done by a machine, would make the accountant entirely unnecessary.

We must distinguish between financial accounting and management accounting. *Financial accounting* is the task of preparing and presenting an accurate representation of the company's business to outsiders, principally the SEC, the shareholders, and government agencies like the Internal Revenue Service. This process is highly regulated, and it is important that

---

* This chapter and the next provide background information about traditional accounting methods and the concepts of world-class and lean manufacturing. Readers who are anxious to move into the practical application of the issues raised in Chapter 1 may want to skip ahead to Chapter 4, which deals with accounting simplification.

the information (balance sheets, profit and loss, and so forth) be accurate and presented according to the regulated standards. The government feels so strongly about this that it will put you in jail if you violate the standards.

Cost and management accounting, on the other hand, is used internally to help the company's managers control and improve the business. Although there are accounting standards associated with these tasks, there is no legal requirement to perform these tasks in any particular way or to perform them at all. A company can do as much or as little cost and management accounting as it wishes, and it can do these things any way it wants. Cost and management accounting are for internal use and must be of value to running the company's business.

As with any non-value-added but required task, it is important that the financial accounting processes be stripped down to their bare requirements and—after the processes have been radically simplified—automated as much as possible. All non-value-added activities must be either eliminated or simplified so they take the minimum amount of work, effort, and time. Fortunately, these are among the easiest of business functions to computerize because they are regulated so strictly. The objective of an accountant in a company moving toward lean is to eliminate the bulk of the regular financial accounting and bookkeeping activities (including accounts payable and receivable) so that his or her time can be spent on the more important issues of analysis and business improvement. (For more detail, see Chapter 4.)

In most companies, the financial accounting systems, manual and automatic, are much too complicated and time consuming. They include numerous manual journal entries, complex accruals and allocations, lengthy matching of invoices with purchase orders, and so forth. The month-end procedures are conducted with Byzantine complexity, and the final reports are often produced manually using homegrown spreadsheets that are pored over for many hours and days instead of being printed directly from the primary computer system. Many of these reports, particularly those concerning budgets and variances, result in lengthy, time-wasting, useless meetings that deal more with assigning blame than creating improvement. This is not only wasteful in itself, but it also diverts attention from the real issues of moving the company toward a lean enterprise.

Cost and management accounting is intended to help companies control and improve their business. Unfortunately, the traditional approaches to cost and management accounting fall down badly as a company moves away from traditional approaches and into lean thinking. The time-honored cost and management accounting methods were developed in the late nineteenth century and early twentieth century to meet the dynamic needs of expanding industries in Europe and the United States. The concepts were formalized by the 1930s and have since been the basis for manufacturing financial control. However, in the last 15 or 20 years, profound changes have taken place in Western manufacturing industry, but the techniques and concepts of management accounting remain unchanged.

HISTORY OF MANAGEMENT ACCOUNTING

The historical development of management accounting is fascinating. Contrary to the popular myth depicting accountants as humorless men in gray suits, the people who were responsible for introducing the concepts of cost accounting were dynamic and innovative leaders. They were among the pioneers of the nineteenth-century industrial explosion.

Although the principles of financial accounting and bookkeeping were developed in the fourteenth century as a method of tracking commercial endeavors, management accounting was not required by the merchants and small business owners of the years prior to the Industrial Revolution. It was the advent of large industrial organizations in the nineteenth century that created a need for information about the financial transactions occurring within these companies.

New accounting methods were developed because entrepreneurs were beginning to hire people on a long-term basis, make long-range capital investments, establish hierarchical company structures, and introduce more complex production technologies. The new decision making within these enterprises required new internal financial information systems.

Early costing systems concentrated on conversion costs for the calculation of cost per ton and cost per unit of straightforward manufacturing processes like steelmaking or gun powder. These costs included labor and materials, and occasionally the application of a little overhead. As communication and transportation improved during the nineteenth century, new management techniques were required to control more far-flung enterprises like railroads, retail stores, and services. These needs brought the development of cost and profit centers, and new performance measures for individual branches.

The influence of the scientific management movement, with its emphasis on a standard method for each production task, led to the introduction of standard costs for manufactured products. The diversified corporations that began to develop in the early twentieth century required the use of budgeting, capital investment analysis, performance measurement ratios, and divisionalized accounting.

All the essential elements of modern management accounting had been established and codified by 1930. These included:

- Financial forecasting
- Budgeting
- Standard costing
- Overhead absorption
- Variance analysis
- Transfer pricing
- Return-on-investment calculations (ROI)

In addition, the integration of the cost accounts with the financial accounts had by that time become accepted practice and was required by the auditors. At the same time, business schools and professional institutions were formed and began to teach "modern" business methods. The techniques of management accounting became established practice.

Since the 1930s, there have not been any significant changes in the techniques of management accounting. Many refinements have been introduced, and a great deal of academic work has been done, but the fundamental principles have not changed. In contrast to this stable picture, manufacturing industry has changed enormously. Products have changed dramatically. Production technology has been transformed, and automation has changed cost distributions. Research and development cycles in some industries are much longer and more costly, and employee needs and aspirations are very different. In short, a revolution has taken place in industry, and the rate of change is increasing every year. Traditional methods of management accounting have not kept pace with these dynamic changes.

PROBLEMS WITH MANAGEMENT ACCOUNTING

The problems with management accounting fall under five major headings:

1. Lack of relevance
2. Cost distortion
3. Inflexibility
4. Incompatibility with lean thinking
5. Inappropriate links to financial accounts

Lack of Relevance

Management accounting reports are not directly related to the company's strategy. Management accounting systems are, by their nature, primarily financial in the way they collect and report information. But the strategic goals of lean companies are primarily established nonfinancially. The strategic goals will often make reference to financial objectives—and these goals can generally be reported through the financial accounting system— but most of the goals are nonfinancial. These include issues such as:

- Products
- Markets
- Customer value
- Quality
- Reliability
- Flexibility
- Innovation
- Time to market
- Lead times
- Customer satisfaction
- Employee involvement
- Social issues

None of these issues is addressed by traditional management accounting. If management accounting does not address the strategic issues of the company, then it is, by definition, irrelevant.

Financial measures are not meaningful for the control of production and distribution operations. Most people in a factory do not think in terms of the financial aspects of their work. Instead, they concentrate on issues such as:

- Production rates
- Yield
- Quantities
- On-time deliveries
- Reject rates
- Schedule changes
- Stockouts

These are the real issues of manufacturing, not contrived financial analogs.

Do the managers or supervisors in your plant get excited when they hear that the management accountant is bringing their monthly variance reports? Do they exclaim: "Wow! These reports are really going to help us improve the process and do our jobs better." Of course they don't. Why not? Because the management accounting reports provide nothing of use or value to anyone in the business operations. In fact, they know that the results shown in the reports are going to cause them a problem because they will have to go to lengthy and useless cost-variance meetings, where they will have to "explain" why the costs are different from standard or some other fiction.

The application of cost accounting to pricing is dangerous. Management accounting analysis has become less significant to pricing decisions in recent years because worldwide competition has made product pricing market-driven and not cost-driven. Indeed, the starting point of lean thinking is *customer value.* Pricing is based on the value created for the customer, and there is no direct relationship between price and cost. Few companies have the luxury of setting their own prices according to an acceptable margin above the product costs. Those days are long gone for most companies.

The requirement is to set the price according to the needs of the market to give the company a competitive edge, and account must be taken not only of the physical product, but also of other aspects relating to

- Customer service
- Additional value-added services

- The long-term relationship with customers
- Intangible issues, such as company reputation, that create value in the eyes of customers

For the majority of manufacturers (other than some defense suppliers), prices are established by marketing decision rather than by analysis of costs. Does this mean that tracking costs is no longer important? Of course not! Lean companies are very concerned about costs. In fact, cost is so important, they need to use much better methods than the traditional standard product costs and variances. Therefore, the accounting tools needed in this environment include the following techniques:

- Value-stream costing
- Box scores
- Target costing
- Life-cycle costing
- Value analysis

(See Chapter 5, Value-Stream Accounting, and Chapter 8, A New Approach to Product Design, for more information on these tools.) The traditional product cost and profitability analysis are not useful in this environment.

Cost Distortion

Traditional cost accounting is concerned with cost elements, but the pattern of cost elements has changed in recent years, and this detailed analysis is less important. Back when cost accounting was developed, the breakdown of costs into cost elements was quite straightforward. Labor was by far the biggest cost element for most products, materials coming next, and overheads were relatively small. This is no longer the case. The average American-manufactured product accrues less than 7% of the total cost from labor, and overheads represent a huge contribution to cost. The traditional methods of breaking down product costs into elements are (at best) irrelevant and often harmfully misleading.

The distinction between direct and indirect costs is not as clear cut as it used to be. The same is true of fixed and variable costs. Once again, in the early days of cost accounting, there was a clear distinction between direct and indirect costs:

- *Direct costs* were directly associated with making the product.
- *Indirect costs* were other company activities that contributed cost but did not contribute to making the product. These included overhead activities like management, product design, sales and marketing, and so forth. These indirect costs were relatively low in comparison to direct costs.

Today, this is no longer the case, and the ideas associated with direct and indirect costs do not apply.

Lean companies emphasize teamwork, continuous improvement, and employee empowerment. These approaches require the previously direct employee to become involved in many activities that were previously done only by indirect people, including scheduling, process improvement, problem solving, interaction with customers and suppliers, and sometimes hiring and firing. Similarly, employees previously considered indirect are in fact actively involved in creating the products and providing services to the customers. How can this be considered "indirect"? These changes blur the traditional distinction between direct and indirect employees and render the concept unhelpful in analyzing and understanding costs. Value-stream costing includes anyone working in the value-stream to be "direct"; and almost everyone in the company works in one value-stream or another.

Similarly, the use of fixed and variable overhead costs is not as clear-cut as it used to be. There are some overhead costs that are fixed (for example, the president's airplane) and have no relationship to the products manufactured. Other overhead costs are indeed variable according to product and quantities manufactured. But the majority of overhead costs have no clear-cut fixed/variable characteristics. For example, the use of electricity may be variable in one part of the plant and fixed in another. This distinction is unhelpful in analyzing and understanding product costs and how to improve the company's operations.

Traditional methods of apportioning overheads can significantly distort product costs. This is the problem of allocating overhead costs using labor hours or labor costs. In the early days, overhead amounts were small and labor hours and costs were high; it made good sense to apply the overhead costs according to labor hours or costs. These days, labor costs are low and overhead costs are high, and companies that continue to apply overheads using labor as the driver are misleading themselves, often with very serious consequences. It is not uncommon for a company to close down a product line because it is "unprofitable," only to find that its idea of profitability was flawed because overheads were erroneously applied.

The issue goes deeper than simply saying that overheads applied using labor hours or costs can distort the company's product costs. The real issue is how can overheads be "correctly" applied to product costs? Some companies take the approach that the application of overheads to products is always misleading and make their management decisions based on direct contribution only. Other companies have adopted the ideas of activity-based costing, where the activities associated with the development, production, and distribution of the products are analyzed and each activity is costed. The product costs are determined by applying these activity-based costs according to the amount of use each product makes of each of the activities. This can provide a more appropriate understanding of product costs, but requires a considerable amount of analysis work to be done. There are countless stories of companies spending many months and thousands of dollars developing an activity-based costing analysis, only to abandon it later because it lacked the resources to maintain the information over the longer term. (The activity-based costing pioneer, Professor Robert Kaplan, pointed this out in his article in the *Harvard Business Review*.)*

Lean organizations do not have much need for calculating product costs. Traditional companies put great emphasis on the calculation of the costs of individual products, and these costs are used for all kinds of decision making, including pricing, margin analysis, make or buy and sourcing decisions, valuing inventory, and so forth. Lean accounting does not require individual product costs for these kinds of decisions. The complexity and false assumptions built into the calculation of product costs makes their use downright dangerous to a lean company. Companies using product costs for these routine decisions will find themselves turning down profitable orders, taking unprofitable orders, and outsourcing items they should be making in-house and vice versa.

For example, consider a company that makes four families of products in one of its factories (products A, B, C, and D), and a corporate financial analyst calculates that product family D is "low margin" and should be outsourced to a low-cost country. How much of D's costs will leave the factory

---

* Kaplan, Robert S., and Steven R. Anderson, "Time Driven Activity-Based Costing," *Harvard Business Review* 84, no. 11 (2004): 131.

when the product family is outsourced? Not much. The material costs will go away and perhaps some labor costs, but most of the (so-called) labor and overheads will stay in the building. How will this impact the other three product families left in the factory without cousin D? The costs of all these products will go up because they must absorb additional costs. The corporate financial analyst will now begin to detect that product families A, B, and C are low margin, and the self-defeating cycle continues.*

The use of standard costs (or other full absorption accounting methods) is a weapon of mass production, and it is very harmful to a lean organization. Lean accounting does not address the cost of individual products, but instead considers the impact of a decision on the entire value-stream's costs and profitability, without regard to the cost of individual product.

Inflexibility

Traditional management accounting reports do not vary from plant to plant within an organization. Similarly, they do not change over time as the business needs change. One of the charms of traditional management accounting is that the reports are consistent across the company, the divisions, and the entire corporation. A single set of numbers controls the whole organization. Although this has aesthetic merit, it does not make sense for a lean organization. An important aspect in the implementation of lean is that each site or each plant is different. They have different products, different processes, different strengths and weaknesses, different problems, and different people. For the management reporting to be of value, it must take account of these differences.

Similarly, plants change over time, and their management reporting must also change with them. Continuous improvement—a cornerstone of lean employee involvement—creates rapid and widespread change throughout an organization. Far greater flexibility and understanding are required. The traditional management accounting reports used by senior

---

* It is noteworthy that lean companies (Toyota Motors, for example) are bringing production to so-called high-cost countries like the United States and Western Europe, at a time when traditional manufacturers are closing factories and fleeing to "low-cost countries" like China. Lean companies purchase most of their parts and components locally. Lean companies manufacture and source close to their customers in order to minimize costs. Traditional companies do the opposite. It is ironic that a patriotic person wishing to buy an American car needs to look at names like Toyota or Honda, because the classic American brands are largely made from parts sourced overseas.

managers to judge success may show that a plant is performing poorly when, in fact, the plant is doing marvelously well and the reports are wrong: they are measuring the wrong items, and this lack of flexibility can become a serious problem when the local managers are working hard to bring their plants up to world-class status.

Cost-accounting reports are frequently received too late to be of value. A lean company needs information on time. The timeliness of information will vary according to the need, but it must be up to date and accurate. Traditional management accounting systems are usually driven by the financial accounting calendar, and the reports come out monthly. The reports often appear several days, or even weeks, after the month has closed. If a report is issued two weeks after the end of the period, some of the information will be more than six weeks out of date. The average age of the information is three weeks. This is not timely and is not useful. In reality, no one in the company really uses these reports to control the business; they are available too late to be useful.

Cost-accounting reports are frequently viewed with disdain by operations managers because they do not find the reports helpful; instead, they often find themselves censured when variances are unfavorable. Operations supervisors and managers face a double jeopardy from the month-end accounting reports. Not only is the information late, misleading, and unhelpful, but they are then expected to explain variances and justify themselves. In many companies, the variance reports are accompanied by long analysis meetings entirely devoted to finger pointing. Operations people associate the cost and management accounting reports (and often the people as well) with another instance in which they have to defend their corner instead of working in the plant and doing something useful. It has been known that operations people may manipulate the figures to "keep the accountants off our backs."

What has this got to do with lean? Where is the added value in all of this? The answer is, of course, that the entire process is wasteful and should be eliminated.

Incompatibility with Lean Principles

Traditional methods of assessing the payback on improvement activities often impede lean transformation. Traditional companies spend a lot of time and effort trying to work out the savings resulting from lean improvement. It is, of course, important to understand cost savings, but the reality is that, for the most part, lean improvements do not create significant short-term cost savings. There are always savings with lean improvement, but the elimination of waste from a process creates available capacity. The real question is: "How can we use this newly available capacity to grow the business and increase profits?"

For example, consider a kaizen event in a production cell that results in the cell being able to produce the same amount of product with two fewer people. Is this a saving? Yes, but will the saving hit the bottom line in the short term? *No.* The two people will be deployed to another area of the business, and our costs will stay the same. If we can increase output and sell more products using those two people, then our revenues and profitability will improve.

Although there are tangible savings from lean improvement, lean must be recognized as a medium-term growth strategy rather than a traditional cost-cutting exercise. A controller or accountant using traditional costing methods will often find that the financial reports are showing negative results when goods things are happening. Where on the financial reports can you see the impact of improved on-time delivery, shorter lead times, or better reliability? Nowhere. Traditional financial reports are just not designed to address the issues of lean.

Similar problems occur with inventory reduction. When there is a significant reduction in inventory, there is also a loss of profitability. For example, when finished-goods inventory is reduced by 50% and half the inventory is "decapitalized" from the balance sheet, the additional costs of this decapitalization fall to the income statement and reduce the company's profits.* If, as a result of lean improvement, the lead time to the customer falls from six weeks to one week, what will happen to our sales when the customers gain confidence in our shorter lead time? The company will lose five weeks of sales, the revenues and profits will fall. The traditional accounting systems have no way to deal with this.

Similarly, when deliveries to your customer become more reliable and your lead times shorter, then your customers will reduce the amount of

---

* If you are not an accountant and this paragraph makes no sense to you, don't worry about it. All you need to understand is that when inventory is significantly reduced, profits go down too. The reasons relate to the witchcraft associated with full absorption standard costing.

safety stock they hold on your products. Once again, there will be a loss of revenue.

Imagine yourself sitting at the financial controller's desk. There are mighty efforts being made in production to introduce lean manufacturing, and the people concerned are lauded for their improvements and cost savings. But from your perspective, all you can see on the financial reports is negative: revenues and profits are falling, and you don't know why. Moreover, you have no financial reports or systems to assist you in understanding the financial benefits of lean change and improvement.

Traditional methods of assessing capital investments lead to the purchase of equipment that is contrary to the needs of lean. Western companies use return on investment (ROI), discounted cash flow (DCF), and other analysis tools to determine the viability and desirability of a capital project. These approaches are based on forecasts and estimates that are often little more than guesses. The analysis almost always results in a recommendation to spend a lot of money on a large, specialized, high-tech piece of equipment that will bring a big payback over a five-year period. The engineers in the company will usually endorse this approach because they always want to work with the best and most advanced machines and equipment.

Although capital investment and the use of advanced equipment are important aspects of the modern business world, a lean organization will assess capital equipment projects quite differently from the traditional approach. ROI and DCF do not take account of such issues as quality, customer service, flexibility, or short lead times. The goal of cross-training the people in the company can be hampered by introducing new machines that require specialist technologies to run and maintain them.

Cellular manufacturing needs smaller, often low-tech equipment that fits well into a small cell instead of a large, central piece of equipment that cannot be included in a cell approach. A lean manufacturer is looking to be able to make very small quantities of customized products—the opposite of mass production. As new products are introduced and production volumes need to increase, a lean manufacturer will often want to gradually increase production capability "just-in-time" for when it is needed. This runs counter to the typical results of ROI calculation, which recommend purchases of large and expensive high-volume equipment.

Cost accounting often causes managers to do wasteful and unnecessary tasks in order to make the figures look good. There are countless non-value-added and wasteful things done in a company to "feed" the accounting system. Most of us have war stories of downright stupid things we have done over the years to keep the accountants happy. The most common scenario is the month-end production push. Many companies ship a large amount of their product in the last few days coming up to the month's end. Some companies in fact backdate shipments in the first few days of a new period to the previous period because they have numbers they need to achieve.

These approaches cause the following problems:

- They disrupt the smooth flow of the operation.
- They often compromise quality in order to get the products out the door (to "move the metal").
- They have nothing to do with a just-in-time approach.
- They do not contribute to real customer service.
- They demonstrate a production facility that is out of control.

If you ask the managers why they are doing this, they will reply that they have month-end shipment targets to meet. This kind of logic has no place in a world-class company. Why should production output be driven by an accounting month-end target? This is nonsense.

Here are some other examples of wasteful activities driven by the accounting systems:

- The manipulation of stock figures to achieve month-end inventory targets
- Falsifying time cards to match labor hours to standards
- "Cherry picking" production to enhance earned hours reporting

And the list goes on. The accounting systems are making otherwise rational managers do stupid and time-wasting things for no valid reason.

Concentrating on machine and labor efficiency and utilization rates encourages the production of large batch quantities. Traditional management accounting systems carefully measure labor efficiencies and machine utilization. This is very harmful to lean manufacturing because it encourages people to make more than they need. A world-class company would plan to make only what the customer requires and ship it just in time to meet the customer's needs. The company would not want to build inventory ahead of time just to keep a machine running or to keep people occupied.

It is better to have low labor efficiency than to build things you don't need. Both of these approaches lead you to large batch sizes, whereas a world-class manufacturer is focusing on small batches, one-piece part flow, and fast changeover.

Overhead absorption variances encourage large batch sizes and overproduction. In a similar way, a company that places great store on overhead absorption will tend to build more inventory than it needs. Worse than that, the people will "cherry pick" in order to build products that garner more overhead absorption than others, creating an imbalance in production and inventory levels. In addition, overhead absorption variance is a measure so complex and opaque that very few people in the company even understand it—let alone see its relevance—so the people are driven by something they do not understand to do things that harm the company and do not serve the customers.

Cost accounting requires much detailed data that is costly to obtain. The cost of obtaining the information required by a traditional cost-accounting system is enormous and unmeasured. Very few companies would be able to measure the cost of their costing system. In most companies, the managers would not think about asking the question because the cost and management accounting systems are so ingrained into the company and its thinking that it is difficult to question them, and almost impossible to simplify and eliminate them.

Included in the costly and irrelevant areas of cost tracking are all of the following activities:

- Reporting of labor hours
- Tracking of job-step completion on the shop floor
- Reporting of materials issued to production jobs
- Tracking of work-in-process (WIP) inventory
- The whole work-order process
- Reporting production completions

Beneath the surface of a complex accounting system is some erroneous theory. The theory is that, in order to control the business, you must track and check everything in detail. The more transactions processed on the computer or in the ledgers, the more the company is under control. We have discovered in recent years that the opposite is true. A lean company creates control within its organization by bringing its processes under control: production, administration, quality, new product development, and sales and marketing. Excellence and proactive control do not come from checking and tracking everything; they comes from studying and perfecting every process in the company by eliminating the root causes of the chaos.

The theme of this entire book is to move accountants away from detailed bookkeeping, tracking, and checking and to give them the tools to help create excellence in the company's operations. As Robin Cooper pointed out, "Just as you cannot inspect quality into a product, you cannot account costs out of it" (Cooper 1995).

Cost accounting reinforces the entrenched ideas and outmoded methods that need to be replaced. A common notion holds that accountants are conservative by nature, reluctant to innovate, and therefore obstruct progress. Such is not necessarily the case. When a company implements lean manufacturing, the accountants are often the people who immediately appreciate the benefits of the changes and participate fully in the implementation.

It is true that in many companies that have been successful with lean manufacturing methods, the accounting systems have not changed as quickly as the production techniques and have become a hindrance to the progress of improvement. Sometimes, the accountants feel it is their responsibility to act as an internal watchdog and validate the changes before going along with them. In addition, cost and management accounting systems are frequently complex and ubiquitous, and it is not easy to modify or dismantle them, particularly in a larger, multisite organization.

Another problem is that accountants have been trained to follow tried and tested accounting practices, and there are no new standards for the role and practice of the accountant in this new environment.* The accounting bodies have been slow to provide guidance or training in these new concepts, often advocating further complexity in the form of activity-based costing, resource consumption analysis, pedantic Germanic accounting methods, and so-called balanced scorecards. At a time when production personnel have been going through significant retraining in the ideas of lean manufacturing, total quality management, and other world-class

---

* The humbly named "Learning Leaders Group," set up at the Lean Accounting Summit Conference in 2005, has developed a rubric for lean accounting standards called Lean Accounting; Principles, Practices, and Tools. This was expanded further in the book *The Lean Business Management System* (Maskell et al. 2007).

methods, there has been little opportunity for the accountants to be retrained in their disciplines.

Inappropriate Links to the Financial Accounts

Too often, the cost accounts are regarded as a subsidiary ledger of the financial accounts. Our management accounting systems must provide support to our business operations, not merely background for external financial reporting. This applies to such issues as inventory valuation, overhead absorption, and accounting periods.

A traditional company had long production cycle times and large inventories and, therefore, it required detailed systems to support the valuation of inventory, raw materials, work in process, and finished goods. In contrast, a lean company strives to make cycle times very short and inventories very low. These initiatives are not taken primarily to save money; they are taken to serve the customers quickly, effectively, and flexibly. As a company moves into low-inventory, short-cycle-time production, there is no need to keep detailed track of materials and certainly no need to track the inventory value in detail.

The traditional idea of posting inventory value across to the balance sheet at standard or actual cost is no longer significant. Inventory values can be posted in macro terms based on receipt costs minus stock issues and scrap. Or the inventory can be valued once and kept the same until something significant changes in the company's business. Or inventory can be valued by counting the number of days and multiplying the cost per day of production. There are several ways of handling these issues that do not require integrating the financial accounts and the management accounts.

Similarly, the full absorption of overhead costs into inventory does not need to be done individually for each product and quantity held in stock. This can be done in macro terms for financial accounting purposes and does not require linking the cost and management accounting system to the financial accounts.

Typical monthly accounting reports are not useful in a lean manufacturing environment. If a monthly cycle is required for the financial accounts, there is no reason why this should be true for the management accounts. Worse than this, in many companies, the confusion is exacerbated by the use of the fiscal calendar quarterly (4:4:5 week) accounting cycle, and some companies have different calendars for production, forecasting, sales and marketing, and accounting. Lean manufacturing looks for simplicity; therefore, tying management accounts to the financial accounting cycles has no value.

An incisive criticism of Western managers is their short-term thinking. Financial accounting supports and feeds this short-term approach. In many cases, these approaches are forced on the company by stockholders, Wall Street analysts, company board members, and the like. There is no reason why the management accounting systems should be included in this short-termism. Lean manufacturers are looking for gradual improvement day in and day out through continuous improvement, and for radical improvements through reengineering entire processes and value-streams. It took the major Japanese companies 30 or 40 years to achieve the world-class manufacturing methods that created a revolution in the West in the 1980s. It often takes a long time before the improvements made through lean manufacturing methods hit the balance sheet and the profit and loss P&L statement; there may be short-term negatives. World-class operations require a long-term strategy.

SUMMARY

Traditional management accounting was developed during the Industrial Revolution and the early part of the twentieth century. The techniques of management accounting have not significantly changed since the 1930s, when industrywide standards were adopted. Enormous changes have taken place in technology and production techniques, and the old style of management accounting is no longer useful. At best, it is irrelevant, and often it is positively harmful.

The primary problems with traditional accounting include:

- *Lack of relevance* to manufacturing strategy, the daily control of the business, and routine decisions like pricing, make/buy, capital purchases, etc.
- *Cost distortion* caused by trying to create fully absorbed product costs, which leads to bad decisions and non-lean behavior

- *Inflexibility* because the methods and reports do not vary from plant to plant and from time to time, and because the reports are too late to be of value
- *Incompatibility with lean thinking* by assessing capital projects incorrectly, concentrating on machine and labor efficiencies, encouraging large batch sizes, causing managers to approve wasteful activities, and maintaining wasteful and obsolete systems
- *Inappropriate links to the financial accounting system,* which causes confusion and makes cost and management accounting information late and irrelevant

QUESTIONS

1. Why do accounting methods need to change from the time-honored techniques of traditional accounting?
2. What changes need to be made in the way financial accounting is done by the company?
3. Why is traditional management accounting irrelevant to a company that is moving into lean manufacturing methods?
4. Why are product costs unhelpful in a lean company?
5. Why does traditional accounting impede progress toward lean manufacturing?
6. Why do most companies tie the management accounts into the financial accounts?

3

*Lean Manufacturing**

Lean manufacturing is a loosely defined term that captures the all-embracing changes that have been taking place in Western manufacturing industry over the last 25 years or so. Prompted by competition from radically better companies, particularly Japanese companies, Western manufacturers have had to take a close look at their business approaches and practices. This has not been easy for many companies. The three decades after World War II were halcyon times for American industry. With rich resources, a well-educated workforce, superior technology, a large home market, and an excellent industrial infrastructure, American manufacturers dominated the world.

These successes were based on the concepts of mass production pioneered so brilliantly in the 1930s by such companies as General Motors. But during the 1970s, vibrant Japanese companies began to infiltrate the American and European markets with high-quality, low-price products with superior designs. Within a few short years, some Western industries (cameras, for example) were largely destroyed,[†] and others (automotive, for example) were radically changed by the entrance of competitors from Japan and other Pacific Rim competitors. What these new competitors brought with them were the ideas of lean manufacturing, built upon the idea that high-quality products could be made at low cost in small quantities. This was the opposite of the American mass-production approach and required a clearly different vision and philosophy.

---

[*] This chapter presents the concepts of world-class manufacturing and lean manufacturing. Readers who are anxious to get to the practical issues of simplifying accounting systems may want to skip this chapter and proceed directly to Chapter 4.

[†] People living in Rochester, New York, are dumbfounded that Kodak Corporation is not just hitting hard times, but its very existence is in peril. Kodak has been making cameras and film in Rochester for 150 years and has brought not only prosperity to the city, but art, music, culture, and health care to the community. It is impossible to imagine Rochester without Kodak.

WHAT IS REAL MANUFACTURING?

The basic ideas of manufacturing are quite simple. Where does wealth come from? Wealth comes from digging stuff out of the ground, heating it up, banging it around, making it into something people need or want, putting it in a box, and shipping it to the customer. Wealth is not created in banks, schools, insurance companies, shops, or service industries. Wealth is only created by making things, and the countries that are going to prosper need to be very good at creating wealth through making things. The issues of lean manufacturing are very important to Western countries because, as the twenty-first century progresses, only countries that have a vigorous and effective manufacturing industry are going to be wealthy, have political power in the world, and maintain the freedoms that former generations fought for. There is more at stake than maintaining jobs and making money.

THE FIVE CRITICAL ISSUES OF LEAN MANUFACTURING

There are five cardinal aspects of world-class or lean manufacturing:

1. Quality
2. Just-in-time manufacturing
3. World-class people
4. Flexibility
5. Customer value

These issues are in a sequence that represents the degree to which these ideas have been implemented in Western manufacturing companies. Almost every company has gotten the message on quality, the first category listed above. This does not mean that they have achieved high-quality products and services yet, but it does mean that most Western companies have clearly defined quality programs at work within their organizations to bring the ideas of total quality management into reality throughout the organization.

It is similar with just-in-time manufacturing (JIT), the second aspect of world-class manufacturing. This may represent many companies with only a crude notion of JIT, but nonetheless it shows that many companies are taking JIT seriously. Back in the 1980s, when just-in-time was a new idea, it was difficult to persuade managers that JIT applied to their company; these days, there is no such difficulty, as more and more companies are introducing the ideas of just-in-time manufacturing in a wide variety of industries and situations. However, the third aspect, which pertains to people, is not nearly so well advanced within American corporations because it is much more difficult to implement and requires a long-term dedication to the ideas of teamwork and empowerment.

The fourth major category is flexibility. With the emergence of so-called low-cost manufacturing in countries like Mexico, the Far East, and most recently China, there has been an increased emphasis on flexibility. Flexibility requires manufacturers to provide small quantities of custom-designed products with very short lean-manufacturing times. To many companies, this represents a huge challenge because it is the opposite of mass production and requires the people in the company to develop fast and effective processes for the design, manufacture, and delivery of their products.

There is a second important aspect of flexibility: the ability to understand customers' needs and react quickly to provide products and services that readily fulfill customers' needs. This again is quite different from traditional mass-production thinking. Mass producers seek to make products in very large quantities at low individual costs. These products are provided to the customer from an inventory (with a relatively narrow choice) of finished products. Flexibility requires the company to have (a) a profound understanding of how its products and services create value for the customer and (b) the ability to adapt quickly to meet the needs of individual customers or market segments.

The last and least understood aspect of lean manufacturing is the focus on customer value. This is the starting point of lean thinking because, if we are to understand how to improve a process and eliminate the wasteful activities, we need to know what is wasteful. Wasteful activities are those things we do as a manufacturer (or distributor, hospital, bank, school, or other enterprise) that the customer does not value. On the face of it, you would think that every business would have a clear idea of customer value, because customers will only pay their hard-earned money for things they value. Yet very few companies have a clear understanding of how they create value for the customers, and even fewer have any formal way to measure and document it.

The next subsections of this chapter take a look at each of these five issues in more detail.

Issue 1: Quality

Quality is a way of life in lean manufacturing. The approach taken to quality is quite different from that of traditional manufacturers, because lean manufacturing is not only concerned with detecting quality problems, but also with resolving the problems at their source. A traditional manufacturer, recognizing that there will always be rejects with any manufactured item, will build acceptable reject rates into production plans and customer orders. In contrast, a world-class manufacturer recognizes no such "reality" and sets the quality goal at zero defects or 100% quality.* This level of quality is achieved through a systematic, long-term process of identifying quality problems and harnessing the entire workforce to systematically resolve these problems.

A traditional manufacturer employs a large staff of inspectors whose job is to check the quality of all materials purchased from vendors and everything manufactured within the plant. Subassemblies are inspected at each stage in the production process to ensure that they "pass." The thinking behind this approach has always been to ensure quality by having the product quality inspected at each stage in the production process by independent, trained quality inspectors, thereby ensuring the quality of the final product sold to the customers.

This approach is not only expensive, it is also ineffective. Many companies have learned that *improved quality* does *not* come from having *more inspectors*. Instead, what happens is that the production staff do not feel that quality is their responsibility if their work is inspected by others throughout the process. The inspection department is considered to be responsible for product quality. This situation becomes untenable for all concerned, as inspectors become increasingly frustrated because they are held responsible for something over which they have no control, and production people are equally frustrated because they have people looking over their shoulders all the time checking up on them and assigning blame when things go wrong.

---

* The popular designation of *6 sigma* has its origins in the total quality movement. The term *6 sigma* represents a level of quality such that the manufactured products have fewer than 3.4 defects per million items. Sigma (σ) is the designation for the standard deviation of defects within the process, and 6σ represents very close to zero defects.

In contrast, a lean or world-class manufacturer places responsibility for quality with the people who do the job. Pride of ownership is fostered on the shop floor because people have both the authority and the responsibility for quality. Craftsmen have always taken pride in their work because they feel the products in some way represent themselves. Much of this outlook has been lost as modern industry developed from craft-based enterprises to factory-based mass production. Lean manufacturers can engender this kind of pride and personal responsibility within the production force and beyond. For this approach to be successful, the people responsible for quality must have the tools, training, and authority available to them to create zero defects. A number of techniques that lend themselves to this approach are widely used, including:

- Statistical process control (SPC)
- The posting of quality results on the shop floor as they occur
- The authority to stop production when problems occur
- Quality circles, where quality problems can be analyzed each day and resolved
- Appropriate education and quality standards that emphasize the importance of quality to the company

Of paramount importance is a standard approach to the analysis and resolution of quality problems within the organization so that every team has common methods for creating total quality management (TQM) within its area of responsibility.

Furthermore, the quest for quality does not end on the shop floor. Every process within the company is affected by the need for zero defects. Because quality starts with a product that is designed for quality, many world-class organizations emphasize quality through the product design process. This change requires a much closer link among the design engineers, the people who make the product, the customers, sales people, and accountants. Some companies, including some of the very best Japanese companies, have developed an approach called *concurrent engineering*, where a cross-functional team (often including customer and supplier representatives) works together to design a new product. The purpose of these teams is to achieve the following goals:

- To design the products the customers want

- To produce them at a price the customers are willing to pay
- To achieve 100% quality
- To bring these innovative new products to market very quickly

These ambitious objectives have been highly successful in many companies. Sales people, marketing people, design engineers, production engineers, accountants, field-service people, shop-floor people, and administrative staff work together in dynamic "tiger teams" to develop new products and launch them onto the market. (See Chapter 8 for more information on concurrent engineering.)

The results have been phenomenal:

- New products have been introduced at a fraction of the time.
- Product quality becomes radically better.
- The design is "right first time" because a range of skills contributing to the design ensures that all aspects are fully considered.
- The company is introducing products the customers want to buy.

Issue 2: Just-in-Time Manufacturing

Just-in-time manufacturing, a cornerstone of lean manufacturing, is another term that has become common parlance in the last few years. JIT is concerned with the elimination of waste, where waste is defined as any activity that *increases cost* without adding *customer value* to the product manufactured or the service provided. The objective of JIT manufacturing is to change the production process to eliminate waste. Emphasis is placed on eliminating inventory, not only because inventory is an expensive waste in itself, but also because high levels of inventory have traditionally been used to hide numerous problems within the company, such as:

- Poor quality
- Poor planning and scheduling
- Inaccurate records
- Poor design
- Unreliable suppliers
- Unpredictable production yields

Another emphasis of JIT manufacturing is on short production-cycle times. Long cycle times require high work-in-process (WIP) inventory. Long cycle times mean that products are delayed in queues, in planning, in WIP inventory, in material movements, and in inspection. All these activities are wasteful in themselves, and they also require complex and expensive systems for tracking and controlling the materials on the shop floor.

In contrast, short cycle times allow you to make today what the customers want today instead of making large batches and storing them in finished-goods inventory. If the production area can be set up to make small quantities very quickly (meaning that the production cycle time is shorter than the lead time offered to the customer), then the company can make to order (with no need for large finished-goods inventory) and can be much more responsive to the changing needs of the customers.

The following subsections describe some of the issues of just-in-time manufacturing.

Shop-Floor Layout and Cellular Manufacturing

Traditional manufacturing plants are laid out by function, with all the machines or workstations associated with a single aspect of production clustered together. A production order is completed by moving the materials from one work center to another as various operations are performed and the batch of product gradually completed. Very often there are subassemblies or fabricated parts that are manufactured in batches and then put into a stockroom awaiting use in a later production work order. This kind of production is very wasteful, because it requires a lot of movement of materials, large batch sizes, queues on the floor, high work-in-process inventories, and a lack of teamwork caused by the division into separate departments.

In contrast, lean manufacturers usually adopt cellular manufacturing methods where all the machines, equipment, and people required to manufacture a product are located *together*. The entire product, or a major part or subassembly, is made in the cell, which offers the following benefits over the traditional manufacturing layout:

- *Cellular manufacturing eliminates the movement of materials* because all the work is done within the relatively small cell. The production is completed in small batch quantities, ideally batches of one (known as single-piece part flow), with very short production-cycle time, because only small quantities are made at a time. For example, the Dell computer I am using to write this book was custom-manufactured to my specification. The Dell company has built its production process around the ability to assemble computers using single-piece flow.

- *Cellular manufacturing also reduces work-in-process inventories* because the batches are small and the cycle times are short, and there is very little inventory queued in the cell.
- *Cellular manufacturing creates teamwork* because the people in the cell must work together as a team to manufacture the products. There is a great deal of interdependency among the people, and the team members are given considerably more responsibility and authority than is usual with traditional manufacturing methods.
- *There is no need for complex paperwork* and the detailed transactions that are characteristic of traditional approaches, because the material is in the cell for a short time and the production process is more predictable.
- *Product quality is improved* through this kind of shop-floor layout, partly because the people in the cell are responsible for the quality of the entire product, and also because the item manufactured in one production step is used immediately by the next person in the process. This means that any quality problems are identified immediately and corrected before large quantities of reject product are made.

None of these improvements happens by magic. The establishment of cellular manufacturing and production teams takes a great deal of careful planning and detailed calculation of the "correct" layout to achieve the optimum production cycle time (or *takt time,* as it is known in the lean vocabulary). Cellular manufacturing can only work well when there are standard production procedures and high levels of training and teamwork within the cell so that the principles of total quality management are fully applied. Nonetheless, cellular manufacturing, in one form or another, can be readily applied to almost all manufacturing processes and invariably creates substantial improvement in quality, flexibility, customer service, and cost reduction.

Setup Time Reduction

Small batch sizes are essential to successful cellular manufacturing, low inventories, short cycle times, and improved customer service. Traditional manufacturers usually make large batches in an attempt to gain "economies of scale." The argument is that it takes a long time to set up a machine or changeover from one product to another and, therefore, a large quantity must be manufactured each time to ensure low costs and high equipment utilization. In contrast, a lean manufacturer reverses this argument and says that setup times must be savagely reduced to allow for the manufacture of small quantities.

These fast changeovers can be achieved by applying the concepts of single-minute exchange of dies (SMED*), a method of analyzing machine setups that allows the operators to carefully examine each step in the changeover process and cut out wasteful tasks and time delays. All production plants have their problems with machines or processes that have stubborn changeovers, but generally changeover times can be readily reduced by 75% to 90% by careful, detailed analysis and minor modifications to the equipment. Cutting a changeover from, for example, 4 hours to 15 minutes makes it possible to manufacture very small batch quantities effectively and at low cost.

Synchronized Manufacturing

The causes of high WIP inventories are large batch sizes, long cycle times, and production queues. Production queues are caused by a lack of balance throughout the plant so that the next work center is unavailable when a batch of product has been completed in the previous work center. Some queues are fostered deliberately so as to ensure that the people and the equipment in the factory always have plenty of work to keep them busy.

In contrast, a world-class manufacturer is concerned with keeping cycle times very short and keeping WIP inventories very low. This is achieved through synchronized manufacturing. When production is synchronized through the plant, the materials and products flow evenly through the production cells and never stop for a moment. The various cells and activities within the cells are carefully planned so that there is a similar cycle time

---

* Single-minute exchange of dies (SMED) was introduced to the United States and western Europe through the books of Dr. Shigeo Shingo by Productivity Press in the 1980s.

at each step in the process. This synchronization ensures that the material flows through the production facility according to a fixed and planned "drum beat" or takt time. When one final assembly cell is fed by one or more upstream cells, the production rates of the cells are synchronized so that, as the final cell finishes one product (or batch of a product), the feeder cell is precisely ready with the requirements for the next batch. This synchronization is achieved through careful planning and cell design, and by *heijunka** scheduling to ensure synchronization and level loads.

Tied into the ideas of synchronized manufacturing is the planned level loading of a cell. When the production requirements are calculated to meet the needs of the customers (again, known as *takt time*), the production rates of all the cells and the delivery rate of materials and components from suppliers are established at precisely the rate required to achieve the final assembly schedule. This way, none of the cells will build inventory, and none of the cells will be delayed owing to lack of materials. Often, small amounts of buffer stock are used (in the form of two or three kanban quantities) between cells to provide some insurance against the synchronization going awry. Similarly, a small amount of buffer of purchased materials and components may be held, but these "safety stocks" are very small in comparison to traditional inventory-management methods.

Inventory Pull

A philosophical difference between traditional manufacturing and cellular manufacturing is tied up with the idea of inventory pull versus push. A traditional company, often employing a manufacturing resource planning system (MRPII), will *push* production through the manufacturing plant based upon the production schedules calculated by the master scheduling system and materials requirements planning (MRP) system.

In contrast, a just-in-time approach allows only the customer requirements to *pull* production through the plant according to the current needs of the customers. No production is initiated until there is a customer order, and the production quantity is set by the customer need—the takt time—for that day. The jargon is to "make today what the customers want today; no more and no less." This approach results in little or no inventory buildup—either of finished goods, work in process, or raw

---

* *Heijunka* is the Japanese word meaning "levelizing the schedule."

materials—because the materials and products are only made when they are needed and only in the quantities currently required. This is the just-in-time approach: supplying and making product just in time.

This is fundamentally different from mass production because the production floor is not driven by a plan; it is driven by real customer needs. Nothing is made to stock: neither finished goods nor interim subassemblies.* Everything is made just-in-time, when it is needed. Subassemblies are pulled from upstream feeder cells when they are needed in final assembly. Raw material and components are pulled from suppliers each day when they are needed. Although there are often a few problem parts that cannot be pulled according to this approach and have to be handled more traditionally, a lean manufacturer will have most production pulled through the plant smoothly and systematically in response to customer needs.

The mechanism often used to facilitate the pull system, and to authorize the production and movement of products and materials, is the use of kanban cards. This method was pioneered by Toyota Motors in Japan and is a simple idea. Instead of having a production-planning system (computer or manual, but usually computer) schedule production, the manufacture of a finished product is initiated by the final assembly cell receiving a request, via a kanban card, to build a quantity to fulfill the customers' orders. The materials and components are pulled from upstream cells and the suppliers by the final assembly cell passing kanban cards to the people supplying the materials. These kanban cards authorize the upstream cell to move a quantity of materials (or subassemblies) to the final assembly cell and to make another batch of those materials if they are required. Similarly, the kanban card is used to authorize the suppliers to deliver a small batch of the material required by the plant.

The kanban card has a standard (but small) batch quantity associated with it, and often the container of the items is designed to hold just the correct kanban quantity. This way, small batches of materials are moved around the plant in accordance with the production needs to satisfy the customers' immediate requirements.

Often, the kanban is not physically a card. The container used to store the items can be used as the kanban by having the information printed

---

* While it is theoretically correct to have no finished goods or subassembly inventories, it is common for lean companies to have small quantities of inventory, maintained visually in *supermarkets* and used to buffer the variation of customer demand. Production continues smoothly because the buffer stock reduces the daily ups and downs of demand.

on the container itself (e.g., item number, quantity, supplying location, requesting location, etc.). Alternatively, an electronic kanban can be used to trigger the supply of materials. Electronic kanbans are used when the supplier is physically distant from the user of the materials, and a computer system or another electronic method is used to pass on and authorize the requirement. Other simple methods like a fax or an e-mail are also used in place of a printed kanban card. Kanban facilitates synchronized manufacturing and inventory-pull production.

Total Productive Maintenance

A world-class manufacturer cannot take a just-in-time approach without having excellent tools and equipment. This does not necessarily mean having the latest and highest-tech machines and equipment (indeed, many world-class manufacturers deliberately use older-style equipment that people can readily understand and use—and is paid for), but it does mean having a maintenance program that keeps all the tooling and equipment in perfect condition and ready for use. This may sound unglamorous, but total productive maintenance (TPM) is an exciting and innovative approach to a mundane problem.

TPM puts the responsibility for machine, equipment, and tooling maintenance with the shop-floor operators, *not* with the maintenance department. As a part of the empowerment and cross-training initiatives, the operators are trained to perform routine maintenance and inspection of their equipment, and gradually they are trained to do more substantial maintenance tasks. The maintenance department ceases to be responsible for maintaining the equipment; instead, they become the trainers, the coaches, and the specialists handling the more complex and specialist repair tasks on behalf of the operations people.

This integration of the operator's activities with preventive maintenance has the following benefits:

- It enhances the effort to make quality the personal responsibility of each person within the plant.
- It encourages a team-based approach.
- It prevents the maintenance department from being a separate, self-contained entity.
- It provides much more timely maintenance, better quality, and lower costs.

5S Industrial Housekeeping

Another seemingly mundane issue that has wide implications within the plant is the introduction of industrial housekeeping, also known as 5S. The purpose of industrial housekeeping is to promote high quality, efficiency, and safety through a clean, tidy, and efficiently ordered workplace. Every employee in the plant is trained to keep his or her workstation uncluttered and orderly. This includes the following activities:

- Clearing out unnecessary items from the area
- Cleaning the area every day
- Cleaning, oiling, and inspecting all equipment every day
- Arranging all tools and other apparatus in a systematic way

As your mother told you: "Cleanliness is next to godliness." There is a place for everything, and everything should be in its place. The purpose of this approach is not to save money on janitorial services. Instead, it is intended to achieve the following goals:

- To make sure everyone has an orderly environment within which to work, because orderliness immediately translates to effectiveness
- To develop a pride in the workplace that instills a quality approach within the employees
- To develop a camaraderie among the employees through joint responsibility for excellence in the company's environment

A clean and orderly work environment sets the stage for the use of the visual management methods that are so much more effective than traditional shop-floor control systems.

This does not apply only to the shop floor. Many companies expand this approach to the clerical, professional, and engineering areas of the company. One company in the American Midwest has a rule that at 3:30 p.m. everyone sweeps his or her work area, takes out the trash, and polishes the windows. Every employee, including the president of the company, does this task at 3:30 p.m. every day. It builds teamwork at all levels of the organization.

Visual Management

There is a deeper need for 5S or industrial housekeeping, the need for visual management. Lean manufacturing companies rely on visual management a great deal. This comes from the simple understanding that human beings respond better to visual information than to computerized reports. If you want to have fast, responsive, and effective processes, you cannot rely on the computer spitting out the appropriate reports; instead, you need to have information that is immediately available at the place where the work is done.*

There can sometimes be a misunderstanding of this—that lean companies and lean advocates appear to be against computer systems. This is quite untrue. There are very important tasks that are fulfilled in lean companies using computer systems, but the importance of visual management usually eliminates the need for many of the jobs done by computer systems in traditional manufacturing companies. Lean organizations are not anti computer; they are pro visual management.

Visual management enables fast and flexible response to customer needs and production problems, empowers people at every level of the organization, and ensures that everyone can work together to serve the customer.

Visual management is accomplished by using:

- Physical kanban cards to drive the production pull
- Visual work instructions throughout the process
- Visual performance-reporting boards in the cells, the support areas, and the value-streams
- Visual signals for identifying and resolving quality problems and other daily issues

Lean companies strive to make their management processes simple and visual, and 5S is required to support this. You cannot have visual management if the cell, office, or work center looks like a teenager's bedroom.

Vendor Relationships

High-quality on-time production requires a high-quality on-time supply of raw materials and components. A traditional company tends to have adversarial relationships with its vendors. In contrast, a lean company

---

* Many companies use the Japanese word *gemba* to describe the method of management by going to the place where the work is done rather than sitting in offices and monitoring the business through computer systems. *Gemba* means "being at the place."

builds partnerships with its vendors. The purpose is to create close relationships with a few suppliers so the two companies can work together as partners for mutual benefit and not as adversaries trying to outwit each other.

These partnership relationships are built on mutual trust and a proven track record of on-time delivery, perfect quality, and an ability to resolve problems quickly and effectively. A vendor's ability to meet the exacting requirements of the customer is tested through a vendor certification program that establishes the criteria for a partnership relationship with the customer. Most certification programs have three stages:

1. Measurement, which is quantitative and consists of measuring the vendor's level of service in the areas of concern
2. A capability audit, which requires that the customer visit the vendor on several occasions and assess the supplier's systems and procedures for guaranteeing quality and delivery
3. Relationship building, a level that is achieved over time when customer and vendor personnel from many different parts of the company visit each other and establish close working relationships; it is upon these relationships that cooperative partnering can be built

There is more to these partnerships than merely quality and delivery. The two companies begin to work together cooperatively to achieve the following goals:

• To eliminate waste
• To perfect the product-design process
• To create additional value-added services
• To create mutually beneficial programs

Among these changes are single sourcing, where the customer guarantees the supplier single-source privileges for a number of purchased items. The customer provides long-term forecasts of requirements so that the vendor can make better plans. The supplier delivers small quantities on a just-in-time basis every day. The supplier delivers directly to the shop floor without an inspection or receiving process. Non-value-added activities like invoicing and receipt transactions are eliminated and the processes simplified. These partnerships secure excellent service, low long-term prices, and mutually advantageous cooperation.

Issue 3: World-Class People

World-class manufacturers invest a great deal in their people; these investments include:

- Education and training, especially cross-training, so that each employee can do a variety of jobs
- Team building to initiate improvement within the company
- Participation in a wide range of improvement and enhancement activities

The end result is real authority and responsibility for employees, as traditionally middle-management decision making devolves to the shop-floor operators and other "blue collar" people.

There is a lot of talk about waste in lean manufacturing companies, and just-in-time manufacturing methods and lean management focus on the elimination of waste. But there is a strong argument to suggest that the biggest wastes in Western manufacturing are the skills and talents of 80% of the workforce. In traditional companies, the majority of work people are (implicitly or explicitly) told to come to work, shut your mouth, shut your mind, and do what you are told. They are not involved in any decision making or business improvement, and they are not expected to understand or identify with the company's broader goals and objectives. They are a pair of hands. It is interesting that in some industries the production operators are even called *hands* and supervisors are called *charge hands*. These old-fashioned titles betray an underlying philosophy that is both powerful and damaging.

In contrast, a world-class organization rejects these kinds of attitudes and recognizes that if the company is to succeed in these increasingly competitive days, then the skills and talents of all the people must be harnessed and focused toward constant business improvement. The shop-floor operators, warehouse people, clerical personnel, field sales and service people, and product designers all must work together to create excellent products and services that provide the customers with excellent value.

The following sections take a closer look at some of the ways that world-class manufacturers invest in their people.

Education and Training

It is impossible to build a great company using ignorant people. I am not using the term *ignorant* as an insult; I am focusing on the fact that the business and industrial world is changing very fast, and to compete successfully, every individual must be continually retrained. As a rule of thumb, a world-class company will invest around 10% to 15% of its people's time in education and training. This retraining can take the form of the introduction of new approaches and new ideas, or new ways to do the things we are doing now better. Education deals with the whys (i.e., the theory), and training deals with the hows (i.e., practical instruction).

This emphasis on education and training is not to suggest that people need training only in new things. In reality, even some of the best companies need a great deal of reinforcement of basic business issues. It is amazing how many companies move into lean manufacturing and just-in-time methods and neglect some of the basics. Their enthusiasm for radical change leads them to neglect the "bread-and-butter issues" like inventory record accuracy, good engineering data, sales and operations planning, and so forth. These traditional, unglamorous skills and methods need to be taught and reinforced.

Even more basic are the fundamental educational requirements for literacy and numeracy. Despite the billions of dollars that are spent on education in the United States and other Western countries, many people in the workforce have not mastered the basic 3Rs (reading, writing, and arithmetic). These problems are exacerbated in companies employing people whose first language is not the business language used in the company. Many organizations have added English (or whatever language the company uses) as a second language instruction to their training options.

It is impossible to build a focused and dedicated team when the people are unable to communicate effectively. This is particularly true of companies that traditionally employed immigrant labor because they were low-cost employees, and they now find they must change the company's culture into a quality-driven, customer-focused, team-based organization. The need for basic education is paramount.

An underlying education program providing basic skills and good business practice is essential, but to move ahead into lean and world-class methods, it is also important for the company to teach its people the new business methods that provide a competitive edge. These include the techniques of just-in-time manufacturing, total quality management, teamwork, business process improvement, and so forth. Most of these methods are very straightforward to learn (but often difficult to implement), and the initial problem is showing the working people in the company that the managers are serious about these ideas. Many people have built up layers of cynicism over the years as their managers have lurched from one "flavor of the month" business fad to another. It is important that the education and training be directly relevant and can be put to immediate use within the plant.

Cross-Training

The building of teamwork and flexibility into a production plant, distribution operation, administrative group, or service organization requires people to be significantly cross-trained. The use of such methods as cellular manufacturing, total productive maintenance, and concurrent engineering requires considerable flexibility on the part of the people within the company so that they can become generalists instead of specialists. This does not mean, of course, that the company will not have experts in certain areas, but it does mean that company personnel must be trained to perform a wider range of tasks.

The starting point for this is to cross-train people to do all the tasks within their work cell. These may be production tasks like welding and assembly, or accounting tasks like payroll entry and accounts-payable invoicing, or administrative tasks like sales order entry and shop-floor scheduling.

Once this cross-training has been demonstrated within their own work areas, it can be extended outside of those areas to other parts of the company. This is where the real flexibility lies. If people can move from production cell to production cell according to the needs of the customers, then they can be truly flexible. If people can move from accounting to sales order entry according to seasonal work loads, then the company is becoming truly flexible.

Transfer of Responsibilities

For the people within the company to be truly committed to the goals and objectives of the organization, they must have some *control and authority* within the organization. If they are regarded, and regard themselves, as "just a pair of hands," then they will not take upon themselves the additional burdens required to become a part of the world-class organization. The old-style company, where all the problems were taken up the organizational tree and decisions were made by a person of the appropriate management level, is no longer effective in the twenty-first century. Corporate downsizing has forced countless companies to eliminate the layers of management within the organization. Unfortunately, many companies have downsized without creating a new culture that gives authority and responsibility to operational people for the daily running of the plant, within the guidelines and policies established by senior management.

The lean organization is usually quite flat: it has few layers of management. Authority and responsibility lie very much at the sharp end of the business: the people who are working face-to-face with the customers, the suppliers, and the competitors. These changes do not happen effectively by accident. The company must initiate a policy of empowering the people within the organization to make decisions and to make changes to the company's operations that will increase value for the customer and benefit the company.

As a prerequisite, senior management must establish clearly understood and widely disseminated company strategies, goals, and methods. The newly empowered workers must know both the direction and the limitations of their power. The empowerment process must be accompanied by significant amounts of training and education so that the people have the skills and understanding to make the right kinds of decisions at the right time. The workers must also be given resources. Empowerment and participation cannot be done on the cheap. The people need time to work on these changes and new approaches; they need training resources; and they often need tools and equipment as well as authority to spend money.

Like any manager, the newly empowered workers within the organization must have the mandate, the ability, and the resources to do what is expected of them. The result of this level of empowerment is impressive. Instead of the company having a handful of tightly stretched middle managers taking care of such issues as customer satisfaction, process improvement, quality, and vendor relationships, the company now has an entire staff of empowered, committed, and motivated people dedicated to creating the company's strategic goals for radical lean improvement through diligence and individual responsibility.

This picture may be a little rosy, and it is clear that creating an empowered workforce is a challenging long-term initiative requiring consistency and integrity of company managers. Like a rose, empowerment is a delicate flower that can easily wilt if it is not constantly and consistently nurtured.

Few companies achieve the highly effective empowerment described above; but many companies have made enormous strides toward these goals and have gained great benefits through it.

Toyota Motor Company calls this "respect for people" and feels so strongly about it that respect for people is considered one of the two pillars of the Toyota Production System along with kaizen—continuous improvement. Respect for people includes:

- Giving people responsibility for their own work
- Allowing people to think about their work and have the authority and responsibility to improve their own work using lean methods
- Providing people with problem-solving tools and methods so they can see the problems and address them effectively
- Forcing reflection so that everyone is constantly learning from the issues and problems that arise

These respect-for-people issues may seem to be rather vague, but the outcome is very tangible: a workforce throughout the company that is committed and empowered to thoughtfully and cooperatively make millions of small changes to increase customer value and reduce costs and waste everywhere. This also leads to superior job satisfaction and commitment.

Teamwork

A team-based organization is employed by the majority of world-class organizations because teams are seen as the best method of harnessing the talents of the entire organization for continuous quality improvement. In a similar way, if authority and responsibility are to be effectively devolved to the people involved in the day-to-day company operations, then empowering teams is often the best way to achieve this.

There are two basic categories of teams:

Improvement teams
Self-directed work teams

The first type of team is an improvement team, which is used to study a specific issue that is causing a problem and, using a standard TQM methodology, research the problem and implement a solution. These teams are sometimes called *quality circles* or *process improvement teams,* or *employee empowerment groups,* or other similar names. The teams may be cross-functional, including people from many different parts of the company, to address a wide-ranging issue, or they may be a team made up of the people who work in a particular cell or work area of the company that is tasked with improvement of their local processes. These teams can be on the shop floor, in the office, in the warehouse, out in the field, or a combination of these locations. Their task is to create improvement using the company's standard improvement methods. Most companies employ a standard improvement method that is a variation of the TQM Seven Steps approach and the Deming Circle known as Plan-Do-Check-Act (PDCA). These methods are summarized in Table 3.1.

The second type of team is a self-directed work team (SDWT), which is a more sophisticated approach to teamwork and requires considerably more skill, education, and training to be effective. The purpose of a SDWT is to have the people who do the day-to-day work in the team *manage themselves* without the need for a supervisor or manager controlling the team's activities. This does not mean that management activities and supervisory tasks are not done; instead, they are done by team members rather than by a separate overseer.

The advantages of this approach are legion. The people themselves are not only doing the work, they are fully responsible for the work and (generally) fully committed to the company's goals because they are solely

TABLE 3.1

Two Well-Known Improvement Methods

	Seven TQM Steps	Deming Circle
1	Select a process to address and describe the improvement opportunity	PLAN
2	Describe the current process	
3	Describe all the possible causes of the problem and agree on the root causes	
4	Develop an effective solution and action plan	
5	Implement the solution and set improvement targets	DO
6	Review and evaluate the effectiveness of the solution	CHECK
7	Standardize the solution and then reflect and act on what has been learned	ACT

responsible for achieving those goals. These teams hire and fire team members, create their own education and training programs, initiate improvement, and so forth. For example, at Saturn Corporation, the car company jointly owned by General Motors and the United Auto-Workers Union, the self-directed work teams have more than 30 activities they perform in addition to their primary purpose of making the products. In addition to creating a more committed and motivated team, SDWTs are also very cost effective because they require fewer people to achieve the same amount of work, and they tend to be very effective at process improvement.

Participation

Woven into all the previous discussions about world-class people is the assumption that the people within the company participate in the company's self-improvement programs. If people's broad skills and talents are to be employed for business improvement, then they must participate. If teamwork is to be effective, the people must participate. If there is to be transfer of responsibility and cross-training, the people must participate.

This participation can be formally or informally organized. If the company sets up education and training programs, initiates teams, establishes standard improvement methods, and provides cross-training, then the people will begin to fully participate if they feel sure the senior managers of the company are serious and have integrity. It takes time for these programs to begin to become effective, and there are always problems, delays, and setbacks in the process, but everyone in the company will begin to participate, even without a formal and explicit participation approach.

More formal approaches have been very successful in some companies. One formal approach is to create a suggestion program. A suggestion program in a world-class company is much more than the cobwebbed suggestion boxes seen around traditional companies. The suggestion programs (sometimes called "just-do-it improvements" or "quick and easy kaizen") actively elicit improvement suggestions from individuals and teams of people within the company. They are a means of transferring good ideas and plans from the people working the jobs day in and day out to the middle managers and quality improvement coordinators.

Very often these suggestion programs are linked into the improvement team activities so that the people can initiate the implementation of their suggestions. These suggestion programs are often monitored carefully so that the number of suggestions made and implemented is known and so that the people and teams involved get the credit. Sometimes the people making the suggestions are compensated based upon the number and success of their suggestions.

Another form of participation is membership of the improvement teams. In some companies, membership is voluntary and monitored. In others, people are assigned to teams. It is essential that people actively work on the team if improvement is to be achieved; lip service will not get the job done. In reality, people are more than willing to participate above and beyond the call of duty if they feel that they are really making a difference and that their voices are heard. It is the job of the company's management to create an atmosphere where people are motivated for team process improvement. This leadership can only come from the top of the company.

Profit sharing is another method for encouraging participation. It is common for lean and world-class organizations to use a formal profit-sharing program whereby the employees at every level of the company get paid bonuses when the company profits increase. There are many varieties of these programs, but they are usually simple, based on the company making higher bottom-line profits, are paid quarterly or biannually, and apply equally to every employee instead of being related to specific job performance.

For example, the Wiremold Company, a well-known lean success story, set a goal of 25% profit sharing when it embarked on its lean journey. It took the company about 10 years to reach this level of profit sharing, but it provided a very real incentive for the people to "go the extra mile."[*]

Issue 4: Flexibility

Flexibility is increasingly important to world-class companies. The market and the customers' requirements are driving toward greater flexibility than ever before. Increasingly, the verities of mass production are violated by the needs of the customers for the delivery of small quantities of more customized products at lower prices.

The genius of mass production was to dramatically reduce production costs and overhead costs in the following ways:

---

[*] More information on this can be found in *Better Thinking; Better Results,* a book by Bob Emiliani.

- By making very large quantities of the same product, by limiting choice (any color you want, so long as it is black!)
- By standardizing production, service, and support activities
- By reducing changeovers and running "economic batch quantities"

This approach is just not viable when the market wants more choice, shorter delivery lead times, and rapid introduction of innovative new products. Unfortunately, many companies have been forced by their customers to produce wider variety and smaller quantities, but they have not recognized that fundamental change is taking place in their business. They are trying to provide this new paradigm of service using the traditional mass-production methods, and this can be calamitous.

The next few sections describe some of the issues pertaining to an organization's flexibility.

Product Mix and Volume

There are wide issues associated with flexibility, but flexibility at its most basic is concerned with the mix and volume of the products manufactured and shipped to the customers. The ideal is to *make today* what the customers *want today*, no more and no less. An important aim of a lean and world-class manufacturer is to set up the production operation so that the needs of the customers can be met immediately without holding large stocks of finished goods. This requires a cellular production capability approaching single-piece part flow so that precisely the right quantity of each product can be manufactured each day and each shift.

The ability to rapidly change production capacity is also required. Cross-training is important because this allows the people to move to cells that have a heavy load and reduce capacity on cells that are lightly loaded. Many companies find that excess machine capacity is required to support a flexible production policy; people can be cross-trained, but equipment is often less flexible. This leads to a capital acquisition policy that favors the purchase of more-flexible production equipment.

Some companies have developed innovative methods of providing flexible production capacity over and above the traditional overtime and extra shifts. This may include the use of temporary personnel that can be called in at a moment's notice. One company employs local farmers to provide temporary production assistance. This is a win–win because the farmers are very adept at the kind of work required, and they appreciate the additional income. The number of people required is worked out by 5:30 p.m. the previous night based upon customers' orders needing shipment the following day, and the company calls in as many people as it requires. There is, of course, an agreement that assures each person a certain amount of work each month, and rotation ensures that the work is spread fairly among the people involved and that each person's skills are maintained and enhanced.

Flexibility in product mix and volume requires flexibility on the part of the workforce and the availability of excess production capacity. This runs contrary to traditional production ideas, where specialization and utilization are valued, but the realities of the marketplace require a significant change of attitude in these areas.

Short Lead Times and Make-to-Order Production

The days of delivery lead times stated in weeks are gone in most industries. The customer, and very often ourselves as consumers, requires faster service. Almost every company is faced with demands from customers to be able to deliver products much more quickly than ever before. Traditionally, if the production lead time was longer than the promised delivery lead time, the company would need to hold large amounts of finished-goods inventory so that the customers could be served from stock. And this approach lent itself to the inflexible large-batch manufacturing methods of mass production.

Finished-goods inventory is no longer an option to solving this basic mismatch between the needs of the customer and the production capability of the company. The need of more customers for custom-designed products, the need for just-in-time deliveries, lower costs, and rapidly introduced new products into the market all mitigate against the use of large finished-goods inventories. To be successful in the new market environment, companies must learn to make products to order and employ very short lead times.

The need for short lead times and make-to-order production requires the use of just-in-time methods, including

Fast changeover
Small batches

Cellular manufacturing
Single-piece part flow
Supplier relationships and certification
A flexible workforce

The needs of the marketplace in most industries mitigate against the use of traditional production methods and require a move toward at least some aspect of just-in-time manufacturing.

The same is true in service and nonmanufacturing industries, where customers are requiring more services in a more timely manner, and at a lower cost. For example, car rental companies have been forced by their customers to provide much better service than before. No longer do you stand in lines to get a car; you can select one directly at the lot. When returning the car, you can check in and have a receipt in your wallet before you have taken your suitcase out of the trunk. The same is true of banks, insurance companies, financial services, food services, telephone service, mail-order merchandisers, and numerous other service-based industries; and electronic communications are rapidly making these services more and more flexible.

New Product Introduction

The other important aspect of flexibility is the introduction of new products. The ability to introduce innovative products quickly and effectively is a key to world-class performance because customers are increasingly requiring more new products more quickly. The world-class manufacturer uses techniques like concurrent engineering to ensure that new products are:

- Designed fast
- Designed for quality
- Designed for manufacturability
- Designed with a focus on the customer's needs

The ability to design products fast and effectively can provide an increasingly competitive edge. For example, Pressure Switches Inc. (PSI) in Connecticut, a manufacturer of aerospace and defense pressure controls, introduced a policy of 24-hour design of custom switches. When a customer requires a custom designed switch, the engineers are able to design, prototype, test, and provide samples of the new switch within 24 hours of receiving the inquiry. This approach has been a key ingredient of PSI's success within a highly competitive and troubled marketplace in the 1990s.

Another example is Honda Motorcycles in Japan, which introduced a policy of launching a major new product every month. The purpose of this policy was not only to provide innovative new products to the market, but also to perfect the new-product introduction process. A process that occurs regularly every month and is a standard part of the business practice can be performed much better than an ad hoc product launch that occurs sporadically.

Issue 5: Value to the Customer

Lean companies have a unique passion for understanding the value they create for their customers; how that value is created by their products, services, and other value-adding attributes; and what they need to do to increase the value created for their customers. Many companies employ astute sales and marketing people who know how value is created using their intuition. But this is no substitute for a formal and rigorous method for understanding customers' needs and desires, and translating those into the 5–10 key value-creating attributes of the company's products and services, and then quantifying those attributes into a clear understanding of how much value the customers place on a product or family of products.

When you have this profound understanding of what creates value for the customer, you can set about making more value. You can price your product correctly. Here is one way to determine how much your products should cost:

Product Cost = Value (or Price) – Required Profit

When you know the true cost required to meet your customers' needs and your company's need for short- and long-term prosperity, then you can design (or redesign) the production and services processes to ensure that your product meets these needs. Lean companies drive their ongoing process improvement from a profound understanding of customer value.

Unfortunately, very few Western companies have this level of understanding of value. Even fewer use this understanding to drive change and improvement. And yet this is the starting point of lean thinking. Most Western public companies seem to focus their attention on value to the *stockholders* or the *owners*. This constant obsession with Wall Street and the stock price—often bolstered by huge financial bonuses for company executives—has led many companies to divert from lean transformation and continue with traditional and wasteful processes.

Having said this, some of the Western companies that are most successful with lean, and reap the highest benefits, have a deliberate focus on customer value. These include The Wiremold Company* and New Balance Athletic Shoe Company.† These companies use the voice of the customer, target costing, and quality function deployment methods‡ to gather the information required to truly understand the issues that are of importance to their customers and then to quantify them.

When the value-creating attributes of your company's products and services are understood, then the engineers can develop products that maximize the value by optimizing the attributes that create the value. Often, the value of a product can be increased by removing functionality and making it simpler and easier to use. This can also make the product less costly to manufacture, distribute, and use. The materials used to make the products can also be changed to increase the customer value or reduce the costs.

The value to the customer may be less within the physical product itself as in the services provided by the supplier. For example, a customer may need a short lead time, and the customer defines "short" as five days. But would more value be created if the lead time were only two days? The answer is "maybe." It is very important that we understand the issues that truly create value for the customers, and which of those can increase value if we improve them. This way, we can make clear and intelligent decisions about where to apply our limited resources for the design, manufacturing, distribution, and marketing of our products. Truly lean organizations place great emphasis on understanding and creating value for their customers.

---

* Emiliani, Bob. *Better Thinking; Better Results.*
† *Target,* Journal of the Association for Manufacturing Excellence.
‡ See Chapter 8.

AGILE MANUFACTURING

So far, this chapter has covered the primary differences between traditional and lean or world-class manufacturing. In recent years, however, there has been a move beyond world-class or lean manufacturing methods into agile manufacturing.* The term *agile* is once again loosely defined, and much of the work on agility has been theoretical rather than practical. However, there are many companies that have moved into at least some of the methods of agility and are reaping great benefit. As we move further into the twenty-first century, the ability to be agile will become a major factor for all companies—manufacturing, service, and infrastructure—that need to be competitive in the world market.

There are four principal elements to an agile organization (Goldman, Nagel, and Preiss 1994):

- Enriching the customer
- Cooperating to enhance effectiveness
- Mastering change and uncertainty
- Leveraging people and information

The remainder of this chapter describes each of these elements in more detail.

Enriching the Customer

World-class manufacturers focus on the customers' needs and ensure that the customers' products are shipped on time, all the time. The lean or agile company goes a step farther and addresses the wider issues of customer value. The emphasis is placed on the benefit derived by the customers from using the products and services the company provides. Companies seeking to become agile address issues such as these:

- Measuring the customer's benefit from the products
- The ease with which the customer uses and deploys the products

---

* The term *agile manufacturing* is losing popularity because the ideas and methods of agility are now included in the general term *lean manufacturing*.

• The ease with which the products fit into the customers' business practice

An agile company focuses not on selling *products* to customers but on selling *business solutions* that create great value for customers. The sale of products is not seen as a single transaction, but as the creation of *a relationship* so that products can be customized or designed to meet the customer's specific need and to provide the highest value. The idea is to provide products of such high value that pricing issues become secondary because the customer is receiving a unique combination of product, service, and value. Product design focuses on being able to continually add value to a product as time goes by. Instead of selling your customers more and more products, you sell them products that can be easily enhanced by additional features or by software additions.

The value the company provides to the customer is less within the products than through the *additional services and added-value information* that goes with them over their life cycles. The organization sells skills, knowledge, and information as much as products. The emphasis is on reconfiguring the products and services over time as the customers' needs change and as the products and their related technologies are enhanced. These skills and knowledge also manifest themselves in an ability to respond rapidly to customers' needs for new products, adapted products, and new or enhanced methods of using the products and services. The agile company will sometimes combine in-house expertise with that of third-party partners with specific skills for specialized needs.

Cooperating to Enhance Competitiveness

The essence of an agile manufacturer is learning to adjust to the changing needs of the marketplace by working cooperatively within and outside the organization to serve customers and achieve the company's objectives. The element of cooperation expands outside the company into third-party partnerships.

The organizational structure of an agile organization will lend itself to a great deal of cross-functional and concurrent activity. This requires excellent communication within the organization and excellent and continuous training of the people. There must also be ready access to huge amounts of information about products, about the markets, about the technologies, about competitors, and about the company. Internal information, good and bad, about the company must be disseminated throughout the organization. There must be convenient ways for all employees to tap into the latest information about customers, products, production schedules, suppliers, new product introductions, personnel issues, financial information, and so forth. The people within the company must be able to make decisions based on true customer value, and not on such issues as volumes and margins. For a company to be agile, its people must be highly educated and highly informed.

Agile organizations prize partnership relationships. They recognize that no company can have all the skill, knowledge, and expertise to serve customers in the most beneficial way, and they find partners to work with. Their first choice is to move into a partnership relationship to serve a customer or exploit a market. These relationships often form *virtual corporations* that exist for a short time to serve the needs of a particular customer or market and then dissolve when the need goes away. These virtual corporations are set up based on trust and respect, rather than on legal agreement. There has to be some legal structure, but the agile company recognizes that successful business ventures are based on relationships and not on contracts. The changing needs of the marketplace can lead a virtual corporation to turn out quite differently from the way it was originally envisioned; the letter of the law is of little importance in comparison to the need for the two, three, or more companies being able to work cooperatively for mutual and customer benefit.

The teamwork that is so important internally within a lean organization extends to the virtual corporation, the factory outside our walls, or the design shop on another continent. Cross-functional teams and concurrent development groups within the various firms involved in a virtual corporation are commonplace because it is the virtual corporations' ability to quickly and effectively meet customer needs that makes it of value at all. The teams work on product development, marketing, sales, raw material procurement, product enhancement, and customer relationships. Very often, customers and vendors become partners with the company to form a mutually beneficial organization, and it is not uncommon for competitors to ally themselves for a short time to exploit a specific need.

There are very serious issues to be dealt with when a virtual corporation is established. Some of these relate to intellectual property rights, others to the trustworthiness of the companies and the track record of success in partnership ventures. There are significant personnel issues relating to the intercompany teams that are established: for whom does each person work and how are people "managed" or supervised? The reasons and objectives of the virtual organization must be clearly understood and agreed on so that each company involved knows what to expect of the other partners and what is expected of it.

It is, of course, the development of the Internet that is beginning to enable agility. While still in its early stages, the Internet allows the communication and the formation of less-formal partnerships and virtual organizations. It also has the potential for making available the information required for effective partnering. The Internet is already enabling the development of thousands (maybe millions) of small, focused "craft" companies that can effectively coalesce to meet customers' unique needs. As the Internet continues to develop, the practicality of agility will increase worldwide.

Mastering Change and Uncertainty

Speed of change is another touchstone of agility. An agile company makes decisions very fast: often the people working closely with the customers and partners are empowered to make significant decisions within the guidelines of the companies' policies and objectives. An agile company will have a flat structure: instead of a hierarchy, there are teams of people working together to achieve customer benefit. The organization of an agile company can change very quickly, and it is constantly reforming itself. In fact, organizational restructuring is built into the company's culture, and the organization is a hotbed of continuous change. Agile companies tend not to have functional departments because they are structured to meet the customer's needs, and these needs are invariably met using cross-functional value-stream teams.

The people who thrive in agile companies are risk takers and internal entrepreneurs. The company deliberately encourages individual and team-based initiative within the guidelines of customer benefit and company values and objectives. The managers in the company function as organizational coaches and spend their time helping "self-starters" within the company achieve their best. Even people who try and fail are rewarded for their initiative. Information is spread widely within the company so that everybody can be "in the know," and power is not centered on a few people with access to information.

A primary focus of many agile companies is the cycle time from envisioning a concept and cash coming into the company as a result of this new concept. The faster the concept-to-cash cycle time, the more agile the company has become. This level of agility requires all of the following elements to be in place:

- A clear, inside knowledge of the customers' needs
- Employees who are empowered to make significant decisions
- An organization that allows employees at all levels to contribute to a new initiative
- The ability of the employees to see the benefits (financial and otherwise) that accrue to the company as a result of a new initiative

Leveraging People and Information

As mentioned, an agile company encourages internal entrepreneurs: they are the people who create the concepts and turn them into cash quickly. They must be nurtured by providing:

- An atmosphere that allows them to pursue their ideas safely
- An atmosphere that allows them and their teams to be rewarded financially and in other ways for their efforts
- An organization that has excellent two-way communication throughout the various areas of the business

The people in a successful agile company concentrate on business improvement and the effect of their efforts on the company's success. They are also essentially team players who like to achieve innovation and success through teams of people (within and outside the firm) working together.

To draw the very best from its people, a company must invest in them. This investment includes a great deal of education and training, a great deal of communication and time spent discussing issues and explaining the company's approach to every aspect of the business, and the opportunity to take initiative and (sometimes) fail. Tied closely to this is the exploitation of core competencies. The company must have a clear picture of its core competencies—i.e., the skills and attributes that make the company competitively strong—so that these aspects of the business can be enhanced and perfected. This way, the company is ensuring that it remains at the forefront of the market.

The use of information is an important element of agility. The fast, electronic dissemination of information throughout the organization allows employees to be truly included in every aspect of the company's business, even if they are geographically spread out. Fast and thorough information enables everyone in the company to treat the customers as their close and personal business partners because the customers are not strangers; the employees all have large amounts of direct information about each customer. Technology has enabled us to be closer to the customer even though we are far away!

Another element is the use of information as a competitive tool. The information content of products can be enhanced so that the company begins to sell comparatively fewer products and a great deal of information. This information can be in the form of:

- Product upgrades or a software component of the product
- Additional added-value information from the company
- Information (like self-diagnostics) built into the product itself that is then available to the customer when it is required

Agile manufacturing is a big step beyond merely world-class methods. As Rusty Patterson, vice president of business excellence at Raytheon Corporation and former president of the Agility Forum, a renowned "next generation" manufacturing think tank, pointed out, "It is necessary to be a lean manufacturer before thinking about the challenges of agility" (Goldman, Nagel, and Preiss 1994). The issues of lean manufacturing must be well embedded into the company's culture for the new challenges of agility to be approached. Agility provides such a level of customer closeness and business effectiveness that it will be the goal of all companies to be agile as we move into the twenty-first century.

SUMMARY

Radical changes are taking place in manufacturing industry as we move further into the twenty-first century. These changes will be led by the needs of the customers and by the changes taking place in technology, the global economy, and social structures. The first and most frightening manifestation of these changes was the bold onslaught on Western manufacturers by excellent Japanese companies in the 1970s and 1980s.

These Japanese companies had developed and perfected what became known as lean manufacturing, which includes:

- The use of just-in-time manufacturing methods
- An emphasis on quality known as total quality management
- New methods of organizing the company around teamwork and improvement
- A flexible approach to the needs of the customer

In the West, the 1980s and 1990s were characterized by companies small and large working hard to address these world-class manufacturing issues and to face this new competition vigorously. Many companies have emerged that are truly world class in their manufacturing, design, and marketing capabilities. Others have retreated further into the traditional mode of layoffs, outsourcing,* and the blame game.†

As we move further into the twenty-first century, the rate of change is getting faster. Customers are expecting more. The old mass-production concepts are giving way to the need to manufacture, sell, and distribute small quantities of highly customized products, with perfect quality, and on-time delivery. These new approaches come under the common heading of *agile manufacturing.* Agile companies do not look at customers solely as people who buy their products; instead, they create long-term partnerships with companies to provide short-, medium-, and long-term solutions to customers' problems. Product design takes on a new role. First, it becomes very fast and is integrated into the production process. But there is also a move to create modular and reconfigurable products that can change as the customers' needs change and as technology changes. These products

---

* It is notable that lean auto manufacturers are bringing production into the United States and Europe—and purchasing components from local suppliers—while the U.S. and European auto makers are "outsourcing" to so-called low-cost countries. The lean auto manufacturers make and source locally so as to be close to their customers and the lowest-cost manufacturers.

† The blame is currently going to the unions, the cost of health care, the lack of government leadership, environmental regulation, and the companies' retirees annoying habit of living too long.

are often rich in information, and are supported by a wide range of new and innovative services that create more added value for the customer.

Often, an individual company cannot fully meet its customers' needs, so we have seen the development of virtual corporations. These are informal alliances between companies that have complementary competencies. They come together to address specific customer needs or particular markets. Companies change the way they are organized and structured so that they can reorganize very quickly and thereby thrive in an environment of rapid and unpredictable change. This ability to change and adapt requires placing an emphasis on employing highly competent and empowered people—those who have rapid and complete access to all information required to serve the customers and meet the company's objectives.

The techniques of lean manufacturing represent the starting point for companies that wish to become agile and meet the challenges of the twenty-first century. It will be a century in which change will be rapid, radical, and unpredictable, and where the global market will give rise to increasingly powerful competitive forces.

QUESTIONS

1. Why is quality of paramount importance to a world-class manufacturer?
2. Which aspects of just-in-time manufacturing apply most to your company?
3. What are some aspects of people management that change as a company enters a world-class approach?
4. What are the elements of flexibility required by a world-class manufacturer?
5. What are the four primary issues of agility?
6. Which aspects of agility would be most difficult to implement in your company?

4

Simplification of Accounting Systems

It is a dangerous undertaking to recommend changes to a company's systems, especially the accounting systems. These systems are often near and dear to the people who developed them and use them. Further, every company is different and has different needs. There is no one way to make these kinds of changes.

Having said that, this chapter presents an approach to the elimination and simplification of the accounting systems within manufacturing organizations. As discussed in Chapter 2, traditional management accounting systems are at best irrelevant to a world-class manufacturer, and they are often positively harmful. In any event, the accounting systems are very wasteful because they require huge amounts of non-value-added work and effort for very little return. One expert takes this argument even further by saying that "I believe accounting has no place controlling how people work in today's business environment" (Johnson 1992).

ASPECTS OF TRADITIONAL ACCOUNTING SYSTEMS

To achieve their goals, accounting systems have numerous cost and responsibility centers replete with cost-allocation methods, often requiring double or even triple apportionment from service centers to production centers, and from production centers to products. These require many transactions being entered into the systems (whether they are manual or computer systems). These transactions, in addition to being wasteful in themselves, are also very prone to error.

Inaccuracy is introduced into systems primarily by manual error. If you want your record accuracy to improve, you must reduce the number of transactions entered into the system. The fewer the transactions, the less opportunity for error, and the more accurate the records will be. This is one of the reasons why backflushing can be an important tool: it significantly reduces the number of transactions. As lean manufacturing progresses, even backflushing will be eliminated because inventory tracking can often be largely eliminated. The traditional approach is the opposite to this. A traditional accountant will say that accuracy is obtained by having people check and recheck transactions, but a world-class company removes the opportunities for error.

Traditional accounting systems are expensive and complex to operate. They require a lot of recording of data, entry of data, validation and checking of data, as well as analysis of reports and results. The production, distribution, and clerical support staffs are forever filling out forms, typing in data, and reviewing reports.

What is worse is that the systems are never clearly understood by the people using them. If the systems are complex and convoluted, then the people using them will not understand them. They may understand their particular piece of the puzzle, but they will not have a clear picture of the whole process. When people are using systems they do not fully understand, they use them badly; they make mistakes without realizing it; and they make poor decisions out of ignorance.

Couple these problems with the dubious assignment of overhead costs and the complex, time-wasting, and spurious variance reporting, and you have a system that is an appalling burden to your organization. It provides information of highly questionable usefulness at great cost.

Why would any company put up with this? The reality is that most companies not only put up with this, they actually think it is the right thing to do. This is like taking a sharp knife and opening up an artery: the life blood of the company is spilling onto the ground.

Stupidity and the Annual Physical Inventory Count

The time when inventory records are *least* accurate is immediately after an annual physical inventory stocktaking, because a huge number of counts have been made and an equal number of entries have been typed in. This process is fraught with error. The most shocking aspect is that the auditors will look at write-up and write-down amounts and accept the inventory valuation if the *net difference* is OK.

This is garbage! The individual stock levels can be all over the place, but the auditors will accept the valuation if the net difference is small. This is a total misunderstanding of what is important. Inaccurate records are a killer, irrespective of the net financial differences.

WHY ARE COMPLEX SYSTEMS NEEDED?

Complex systems make sense for companies that are manufacturing in traditional ways, for the following reasons and in these scenarios:

- If inventory levels are high, particularly work-in-process inventory, then complex systems are required to keep track of what you have and where it is going.
- If cycle times are long, it is important to have a system that enables you to monitor the progress of each job in the shop and to give your customers progress reports on the likelihood of completion on time.
- Traditional approaches to quality, which allow for tolerances and scrap factors in production and procurement, require complex systems to monitor the losses and compensate for the variability of the process. This in turn leads to high inventories because additional quantities of raw materials, subassemblies, fabricated parts, and finished products are required.
- If the production processes are complex and materials are frequently moved from one work center to another, if there are backlogs and bottlenecks throughout the production process, and if there are queues on the shop floor, then complex systems are required to keep track of the jobs flowing (or stumbling or lurching) through the production plant.
- A company that attempts to monitor the productive output of individual people will require a complex job-tracking and labor-reporting system, as will an organization that the managers try to control using financial reports, because the detailed financial information needs to be collected, collated, and disseminated.

- Firms that manufacture products in highly regulated industries will require complex tracking systems, as will companies whose customers require detailed costing and quality inspection information. For example, defense equipment manufacturers and other government suppliers frequently require complex reporting systems to provide the government agencies with the detailed tracking information they demand.

THE LEAN MANUFACTURER

As described in Chapter 3, lean and world-class manufacturing organizations differ from traditional manufacturers because they eliminate the need for complex accounting systems by eliminating the issues that require detailed tracking and monitoring of the production process. In contrast to a traditional manufacturer, a world-class company has

Low inventories
Short cycle times
Low scrap
Simplified processes
Synchronized manufacturing
No need for detailed tracking and recording

Low inventories are the result of many different initiatives that come under the broad heading of just-in-time manufacturing, including

Small batch sizes
Fast setups (or changeovers)
Accurate records
Very low scrap
Reliable vendors
Balanced production flow

Short cycle times are similarly the result of excellence in many areas, including

Low inventories
Small batches
Lack of bottlenecks
Synchronized and balanced flow
Making to order instead of to forecast
Very high quality.

Cellular manufacturing does much to simplify the systems and shorten the distances materials are moved. The use of production cells reduces the number of departments and cost centers and simplifies production planning and control methods. This simplification, coupled with shorter cycle times, removes the need for tracking and recording material movement and production steps.

Organizing by value-stream is a big step toward simplification. Instead of cost, performance, and other information collected for each department or cell, it is collected by value-stream. For example, a company that formerly had 150 departments and cost centers may only have four or five value-streams. If we report costs and profitability by value-stream, we have not only a simple accounting system, but also clear responsibility for those costs and profitability: the value-stream manager.

What is a value-stream? A value-stream includes all of the things we do to create value for the customer, organized as a team and accountable for performance and profitability. There are two primary kinds of value-stream:

1. *Order-fulfillment value-stream*: This is organized around the flow of *material* through the production and distribution processes. Order fulfillment follows this sequential course: from the sales process, through customer service, to configuration, to purchasing, to production (together with all the processes supporting production, like maintenance, quality, materials handling, etc.), to shipping, to installation, to invoicing, and finally to cash collection.

2. *New-product-development value-streams*: These are organized around the flow of *information* required to design and introduce new products into the company's processes. These value-streams follow this sequential course: from the identification of customer or market needs, through the understanding of those needs and the value of the new product, to the design and testing of the product, to the

introduction of the product into the market, and into production and distribution.

A value-stream organization—which may be formally organized or created using "dotted line" reporting—achieves the following benefits:

1. It provides clear focus and accountability, leading to faster and better lean improvement.
2. It allows for an empowered and team-based workforce.
3. It is fundamentally lean because it addresses the full flow of the process, from obtaining the materials to the delivery and payment for the product.
4. It fosters creative problem solving by the team members.
5. It provides an environment for the development of lean-thinking managers.

Higher quality of the products and processes, improved accuracy of information, and just-in-time supplier deliveries make inventory planning easier. Making to *order* rather than making to *forecast* is achieved because manufacturing cycle times are reduced. Any company making to forecast must hold extra inventory because the forecasts are always wrong; making to order reduces inventory.

World-class manufacturers treat their people differently. The emphasis is on teamwork, cross-training, and flexibility. Instead of the traditional hierarchical management structures, authority and responsibility are given to teams who are providing products and services to the customers through manufacturing, distribution, design, and administration. The organization is flattened, with everyone having personal responsibility for quality and serving the customer. People are cross-trained so they can make a more flexible contribution to the organization. Cross-functional teams are established to solve problems, design products, and to meet customers' needs. Under this approach, the detailed monitoring of individuals is nonsense, and the distinctions between direct and indirect labor are hazy and unhelpful, as are the ideas of fixed and variable costs.

Low inventories, short cycle times, and cross-trained work teams dedicated to customer service result in great flexibility and responsiveness to customer needs. This characterizes world-class manufacturing more than any other single feature. The entire organization is built around the idea of fast and flexible customer service. Complex accounting systems play no role in this environment.

NEW ACCOUNTING GOALS

The accounting goals of a lean manufacturing organization include paring the accounting systems down so they provide only relevant information and require a minimum amount of effort to obtain the information. This is achieved by

- Radically eliminating wasteful accounting processes
- Aligning cost centers by value-stream to fulfill the organization's information needs
- Provide information for effective decision making
- Reducing the number of transactions

Another primary goal of the accounting systems in a world-class manufacturing organization is to provide information that helps to improve the quality of products and services, reduce the variability of the processes, and enhance customer service. This is a different way of thinking about accounting information. A traditional company regards the accounting information, and particularly the performance measures, as ways of *monitoring people* to ensure they are meeting objectives and budgets. The new approach to management accounting sees the information as the *servant of the people* in the quest for manufacturing, distribution, and customer service excellence.

When this is done, the accounting system can provide valuable information yet be much less costly and wasteful. The information is more understandable because it relates directly to the way the products are made and services provided. The elimination of complex systems, and particularly the elimination of transactions, immediately makes the data more accurate and pertinent.

A spin-off is that simplified systems are easier for people to understand, and when people understand the information, they can make better use of it. Complex systems produce baffling reports and information that creates confusion instead of enabling people to improve the processes. Simplification creates clarity and visibility, which in turn creates understanding. This understanding fosters improvement.

The accounting information must be relevant, minimal, clear, and visible, and it must foster improvement. These are the goals of the new approach to accounting within a world-class manufacturing organization.

A FOUR-STAGE APPROACH TO SIMPLIFICATION

It is usually difficult to extricate a management accounting system from a traditional organization. But as the organization goes through the process of introducing lean change, the simplification of the accounting systems must follow the changes taking place on the shop floor, in the warehouse, and in the office. The next sections of this chapter describe a four-stage approach to the elimination of wasteful and complex management accounting methods. These changes can be made when value-streams, just-in-time manufacturing, total quality management, and other lean methods are introduced.

This suggested approach will not be right for every company. It is given as a logical approach to accounting simplification that is congruent with the thinking of lean and world-class companies. It is also intended to be a radical approach. Each organization must develop its own approach and implement the changes at a pace consistent with the company's world-class goals. The rest of this chapter describes each stage in detail.

Stage 1

Stage 1 encompasses the following tasks:

- Eliminate labor reporting
- Eliminate variance reporting
- Reduce cost centers

Eliminate Labor Reporting

In the modern manufacturing environment, labor content is very small for the majority of products. A labor content of around 7% of the total product cost is typical in Western manufacturing, when all the direct costs and overheads are taken into account. Many manufacturing companies show a higher percentage than this because the overheads included in the manufacturing standard costs do not include overheads outside of the manufacturing area. When all the overheads are included, the labor costs are very low indeed. In some industries—for example, electronics manufacturing—the labor content can be even lower than this.

Traditional manufacturers track labor costs in great detail. Every job step of every production job is carefully recorded and labor variances calculated. This requires that production people—usually supervisors—fill out detailed time cards showing who worked on which job, how much time they spent on setup, production, rework, break times, and so on. This information is carefully collated and entered into the cost-accounting system by a data-entry clerk within the accounting department.

Often, this is linked into the payroll system so that people can be paid according to the number of hours they worked. In companies where people are paid for production, the number of hours and the amount of product they produced (at standard cost) is recorded and wages are set based on this information. This elaborate, detailed, and expensive system is in place to keep careful track of less than 7% of product costs. It is nonsense to do this and it should be eliminated immediately. It provides an illusion of control and in fact is merely a wasteful exercise in futility.

The tracking of detailed labor hours is nonsense for a traditional manufacturer. It is even more unnecessary for a company moving into world-class manufacturing, which operates so differently from the traditional labor-reporting environment in the following ways:

- A lean manufacturer builds value-stream teams of people working together and focused on customer needs.
- Small batches and low inventories are important to a lean manufacturer.
- Short cycle times and flexibility require fast throughput of production.
- Productivity is measured in terms of total products shipped to the customers.
- The distinction between direct and indirect personnel is broken down. Anyone working in the value-stream is considered to be a "direct" employee irrespective of whether he or she makes product, provides engineering support, or places purchase orders. The idea of direct and indirect is firmly based in traditional thinking and has no place in lean.

- The tracking of individual production is harmful in a team-based workplace. It is the team that matters, not the individual activities.
- Tracking individual labor productivity leads people to produce large batches and build inventory.
- There is no time to track the detailed labor used.
- The traditional direct labor productivity calculation of standard hours and earned hours is irrelevant and harmful.
- Tracking the direct and indirect activities of the people becomes confusing, complex, and meaningless.

It can be difficult to eliminate direct labor reporting when there are established work agreements to pay people according to productive time or output. Very often, traditional union contracts set people's pay levels using a detailed tracking system. These approaches must be renegotiated and better methods developed for paying people and for providing a profit plan in line with the company's world-class goals. Most lean manufacturers eliminate the concept of direct and indirect people.

As detailed tracking of labor costs are eliminated, it continues to be possible to track *total* labor costs from the payroll system into the financial accounts. These total labor costs can be used to report the cost of sales and inventory valuation information required on the balance sheet and P&L (profit and loss) report. But it is not necessary to track the jobs in detail to provide correct financial accounting information.

Eliminate Variance Reporting

Traditional systems require the entry of detailed labor and material usage information to each production job so that variances from standard can be calculated and reported. This kind of reporting is the opposite of what is useful within a world-class manufacturing environment.

In a traditional approach to management accounting, variance reports had two purposes:

To correctly value work-in-process inventory
To track poor productivity

It has been suggested that the reason why computer-printed variance reports are so thick (often four or five inches) is because they can be used to inflict grievous bodily harm on production supervisors who have not reached standard. This suggestion was made by someone lacking the usual reverence reserved for variance reports.

Competition—Grand Prize

A valuable prize will be sent to the first reader who can provide a single valid purpose for an Overhead Absorption Variance Report.

E-mail all entries to the author at bmaskell@maskell.com.

None of these issues applies in a world-class manufacturing environment. Work in process is not tracked because the cycle time is so short and inventories so low that it is not necessary. The work-in-process inventories cease to be material from an accounting perspective. Similarly, the issues relating to productivity, scrap, and waste are tracked and solved by the shop-floor people at the time they occur. You cannot wait until the variance reports are printed to take action on quality or a process deficiency.

Variance reporting always was a fruitless, futile, time-wasting task. In a world-class manufacturing environment, it is pointless and misleading and should be immediately abandoned.

Reduce Cost Centers

The traditional company with its hundreds of cost departments and centers requires a complex and convoluted system to keep track of the transactions associated with each cost center. As a company moves into cellular manufacturing and value-stream organization, the number of cost centers is dramatically reduced. Costs are no longer collected in detail by departments and cost centers; instead, they are collected by value-stream.

The issue is not that costs should be collected by the value-stream; in contrast, costs should be collected (if they are collected at all) according to the needs of the manufacturing managers. The accounting system is the *servant* of the production, distribution, design, customer service, and other departments. The gathering of information must be aligned with the information needs of the organization.

Nonsense and Ridiculous Nonsense

This is a quotation from a standard accounting textbook:

Whilst the principle of variance is simple, considerable complications arise in analyzing the variances and bringing out the different factors which have contributed to an overall variance. For example, the wages variance may be capable of many combinations of the following variances: rates of pay, substitution, gang, overtime, conditions, extra rate allowances, revisions, idle time, efficiencies, etc. The other main variances are materials (price, usage, mix), expenses (price, usage efficiency, capacity, volume, calendar) and yield. In addition to these there will be variances due to changes in methods and revisions to the standard during the accounting period. Since all standards are interlocking, it is not possible to make a complete overhaul of the system every time a method changes. Thus, the old standard is retained and part of the variance attributed to methods changes and revisions.

Is this nonsense or what? How does this help you serve the customer better?

Stage 2

Stage 2 encompasses the following tasks:

- Eliminate detailed job-step reporting
- Eliminate work-in-process (WIP) inventory reporting
- Establish backflushing

Eliminate Detailed Job-Step Reporting

Manufacturing companies with long cycle times and high work-in-process inventories require detailed reporting of each production job step because the production jobs are on the shop floor for a long time. If the jobs are in production a long time, it is necessary to be able to track where each job is. The company needs to know this, and the customers will often inquire about the progress of their jobs.

High inventories require detailed tracking because of the value of the inventory. A company has a responsibility to keep track of its assets. The auditors will require a clear understanding of the value of work-in-process inventory as it passes from one job step to another.

As a company moves into cellular manufacturing, however, cycle times are reduced, batch sizes get small, and WIP inventories fall. Therefore, it is no longer necessary to track the detailed job steps individually because the products are made quickly. The value of inventory is small and does not need to be separately recorded. The manufacture of the product occurs within one (or a few) production cells instead of trailing around a circuitous route on the shop floor from one work center to another. There is no need to keep a step-by-step tracking.

The elimination of detailed job-step reporting very much simplifies the shop floor control processes because there is now very little reporting to be done. The product is reported only when it is completed, and not at interim stages in the production process. Gone are the job cards and their associated data entry.

Eliminate WIP Inventory Reporting

High work-in-process inventories require detailed reporting of material movements. In the same way that job-step tracking can be eliminated as cellular manufacturing and short cycle times are introduced, so WIP inventory reporting can be eliminated when low inventories and fast throughput are established.

A traditional company must record the transfer of component and raw material inventories to the shop floor ready for production. As the product is manufactured, its progress is monitored and the actual use of materials reported. This leads, in turn, to material variance reports. When the material moves through the plant more quickly and when the value of WIP inventory is low, it is not necessary (or even possible) to keep track at this level of detail.

The first step is to eliminate WIP inventory. Instead of showing raw material, WIP, and finished products inventories, the company can report raw material and finished products only. The next step is to go to a "four wall" inventory that does not differentiate between the different kinds of inventories. There is so little material that it is shown just as "inventory."

If the detailed reporting of shop-floor issues can be eliminated, the inventory control system is greatly simplified. The hundreds and thousands of transactions that used to be required can now be eliminated together with the time, energy, and confusion these transactions produced. If it is necessary to know the value of WIP inventory for any reason, there are two approaches that can be taken:

1. One approach (used by Harley-Davidson Motor Company) is to have the production process so under control that WIP inventory is always much the same. WIP can be estimated once a year, for example, and will not change substantially because the production process is balanced.
2. Another approach is just to count it. This approach is taken by some Hewlett-Packard divisions. The WIP inventory is so low that it is not a difficult task to count it when required.

Establish Backflushing

Tied in with the elimination of WIP inventory tracking is the use of back-flushing. Backflushing is used when an item (or batch of items) is completed by a cell. The cell reports the completion of the product. The backflushing program does (at least) three things:

- It reports the completion and books the item into finished goods.
- It updates the production schedule.
- It backflushes the components and raw materials.

The component backflush is achieved by reading the bill of material (recipe or product structure) for the manufactured product. The quantity required of each component is multiplied by the quantity completed of the product to determine how much material must have been used. The inventory transactions required to "move" the components from raw material into production are then created in the computer system. These transactions update the inventory levels so that the material planning systems are up to date and, if required, material costs can be posted to the cost-accounting system. If there has been any component scrap or if there have been substitute components used, these must be reported so that the backflush is accurate.

Backflushing substantially reduces the inventory transactions reported by the system. For example, a product containing 30 components would, under a traditional system, require at least 31 material movement transactions: one for each component and one for the completion of the finished product.

In contrast, when backflushing is used, only one transaction is required because the component transactions are all handled automatically.

The bills of materials must, of course, be accurate for backflushing to be successful. But even when the bills are not perfect, backflushing is still more accurate than manually entering all the component transactions because there is far less opportunity for error. Only one transaction is manually entered into the system: the backflushing transaction. All the other transactions are automatic and are therefore as accurate as the bills of material. Backflushing is a powerful tool that is used by virtually all world-class manufacturers. Later we will want to eliminate backflushing also, but it can be a helpful starting point.

Stage 3

Stage 3 encompasses the following tasks:

- Eliminate work orders
- Eliminate month-end reporting
- Eliminate integration with financial accounts
- Eliminate budgeting

As we move into Stage 3 of this simplification process, we have reached the point where the ideas of world-class manufacturing are really beginning to have a radical effect on the way we look at management accounting. We have dismantled most of the tried-and-true features of the cost-accounting system and replaced them with simplified processes. Therefore, we can now move on to changing the structure of our accounting processes.

Eliminate Work Orders

Most manufacturers use work orders to track production on the shop floor. A work order is created (usually by the computer system) every time a production job is required. The work order authorizes the job to be done, schedules the job in the MRP (manufacturing resource planning) system, and is used to track the progress of production for the job. The use of a work order reflects a "job shop" style of manufacture, with discrete quantities manufactured by a specific date, often through a complex series of production steps.

The use of work orders becomes an impediment to a world-class manufacturer. As batch quantities become smaller, more and more orders are required. The elimination of labor tracking and job-step tracking means that work orders are no longer needed to track that information. The elimination of variance reporting means that we no longer need to keep detailed costing information for each job, and a work order is not required to track the variance information.

As small batch, short cycle time, cellular manufacturing becomes the normal manufacturing method, the company becomes more like a repetitive manufacturer than a job-shop manufacturer. Although the products may vary considerably, the production processes are repetitive. A more repetitive style of production planning and control is needed. Work orders should be eliminated and replaced by rate-based scheduling or no scheduling at all.

Rate-based scheduling is similar to that used by repetitive manufacturers. Production cells are scheduled according to the rate of manufacture of products on the cell rather than scheduling a specific quantity on a specific date using a work order. The rate of production is synchronized with the rate of customer demand: in other words, *make* today what the customers *order* today.

Scheduling can be eliminated completely when the production plant and individual cells are very responsive to customer needs. When product mix and volume can be varied quickly and easily, the final assembly cells can be loaded directly from customer orders, and no separate scheduling is required. The loading of production cells that feed the final assembly is achieved using a "pull" approach: that is, components and subassemblies are pulled from the feeder cells to the final cell according to need. Similarly, raw materials from suppliers are pulled each day according to the needs of the feeder cells.

The elimination of work orders using kanban cards simplifies the production process considerably, in the following ways:

- It eliminates the need for tracking and reporting work order numbers throughout the production process.
- Product completions can be reported merely by the product number and the quantity; no additional data is required.

The elimination of work orders also simplifies the computer systems. Production is initiated by kanban or directly by customer orders, and the processes are controlled visually without the need for complex reporting.

Eliminate Month-End Reporting

There is nothing magical about a month-end as far as production is concerned. Yet most companies ship the majority of their products in the last few days of the month. Why is this? It is because the production people are driven by the financial accounting calendar. The financial accounting calendar is used to develop month-end budgets for production, costs, and sales. These are the driving forces. Each manager is judged according to his or her performance against these budgeted targets.

These ideas are a million miles away from world-class manufacturing. A lean production plant has a steady flow of synchronized production that matches customer needs to production capacity. There is no "month-end push." A traditional company will force a lot of products out of the door at month-end, often compromising quality, paying for extra overtime, and creating the disruption and confusion associated with expediting. A lean company does not do this.

The idea of month-end reporting of production results is harmful to companies that are driven by these results. The month-end closing of the financial accounts may have some validity to the stockholders, the Securities and Exchange Commission, or the tax man; but it has nothing at all to do with world-class manufacturing.

The reporting of production information needs to be aligned with the needs of the manufacturing managers, the improvement teams, and the customer. These will vary according to the products made and the market the company is serving. Different kinds of production reporting will be required at different times. Some will be needed continually, either by shift or daily, and others at another time interval. The monthly reporting cycle is irrelevant and should be ignored.

Lean companies are well-planned companies. They use (typically) monthly planning processes like sales, operations, and financial planning (SOFP), whereby the expected customer demands over the next 12–18 months are compared with the available capacity. These sales forecasts and capacity forecasts take account of the best and most reliable information available to the company, including customer information, market intelligence, and internal information.

One outcome of the SOFP process is a series of financial forecasts by value-stream that are then rolled up across the whole plant, division, or company. The month-end results for this month are calculated during the first week of the month. When these forecasts become valid and accurate, the month-end close becomes unnecessary and can be replaced with a less arduous "soft" close—at least for the month ends that are not 10Q or 10K months.*

Eliminate Integration with the Financial Accounts

Management accounts are traditionally integrated with the financial accounts for the purposes of inventory valuation and establishing the periodic cost of sales reporting. This is no longer relevant in a world-class manufacturing company and should be abandoned. The financial accounts are, of course, still required because third parties require them each month or each quarter. However, the management accounts do not need to be tied to the financial accounts.

When inventory values are low and the production process is under control, it is not necessary to link the management accounts to the financial accounts for inventory valuation purposes. When you move to a "four wall" inventory and eliminate WIP inventory reporting, the valuation of inventory on the financial accounts can all be done in macro terms. It is not necessary to calculate the individual costs of each product and subassembly because the value of inventory will be the net of the sales going out and the materials coming in. The overhead allocated to the products is the total amount of overhead expenses accrued during that period. It is not necessary to calculate overhead allocation variances for individual products and sum those up to the balance-sheet valuation.

There is no value to integrating the management accounts and the financial accounts. Each is serving a different purpose, and linking them is irrelevant. The *management* accounts should not be driven by the needs of the *financial* accounts. Instead, they should be driven by the needs of the manufacturing people and the customers.

---

* 10Q and 10K are the designations of the reports required by the U.S. Securities and Exchange Commission (SEC) for a public company's quarterly and year-end submissions.

Having said that, lean companies do not use two reporting systems or parallel financial systems. The methods of value-stream costing* provide simple financial reports that can be used for both internal management accounting and external financial reporting without creating the problems caused by traditional financial systems.

Eliminate Budgeting

Most companies go through a ridiculous ceremony each year known as *budgeting*. A large corporation has a budgeting department whose sole responsibility is to be the master of ceremonies at this charade. If a company's top managers added up the cost of developing the annual budgets, they would fall down with shock. It is not only the cost of the budgeting people themselves; it is also the cost of the time wasted by each manager and supervisor working on the budgets for their own departments, plus the time spent during the year fiddling the results to match the budgets instead of getting on with manufacturing product, improving quality and customer service, and creating wealth.

Every company requires a top-level macro budget. This is needed to plan the company's business direction, determine cash flow, explain the company's strategy to the investors, and provide for capital projects. What the company does *not* need is a detailed budget at the plant, department, and cost-center levels.

If you read the accounting textbooks, you would think that detailed budgets are developed so that costs can be understood and controlled. You would have the impression that a budget enables the company to keep track of its performance and to steer each department in the way it should be going during the following year. However, the reality is this:

- Budgets waste a huge amount of time.
- Budgets are thrown together using spurious information.
- Budgets drive people to do the wrong things.
- Budgets are arbitrarily cut and adjusted by senior managers.

How often have departmental managers labored to create "realistic" budgets for their department's activities, only to find that an edict from

---

* See Chapter 5.

above forces them to trim 15% or 20% from all their figures? Why is it that department managers do their best to adjust their month-end results to match the budget, often at the expense of common sense and even (dare I say it) truthfulness? It is because a budget variance will require them to make reports, attend meetings, argue their case, and generally give them a hard time. Why is it that many budget amounts are spent in the last few weeks of the year? It is because managers know that if they do not use their budgeted amounts, they will be reduced next year.

Many approaches have been devised to improve budgeting, for example:

- *Zero-based budgeting* is intended to eliminate the way this year's budget is a mirror of last year's.
- *Variable budgeting* takes account of the effects of unforeseen changes in the budget expenditure.

There are other refinements of the standard budgeting process, but all of these are merely "perfuming the pig." Detailed departmental budgeting in operational departments is nonsense and should be thrown out.

In contrast, lean organizations use a monthly sales, operations, and financial planning (SOFP) process to provide financial forecasts. These forecasts typically show monthly information about the financial outcome of the company's sales and operations plans for each value-stream, plant, or division over a 12–18-month period. The SOFP financial forecasts are compiled using the most up-to-date and valid information known within the company. The SOFP financial forecasting is not a separate process; it is a part of the regular monthly planning.

The objective of a world-class manufacturer is to improve the quality of the products and services provided to the customers. This is achieved through the detailed understanding of the production or service processes and the elimination of waste within those processes. If you want to save cost, have your people become committed to process improvement, 100% quality, and customer satisfaction. This requires a step of faith. The step of faith is that, if you take care of the right things, the costs will take care of themselves. I am not saying that costs should be ignored, but they should be placed in the correct perspective in relation to quality and customer service.

This is a different way of thinking for many corporations. Management by the numbers may have been okay in the 1950s and 1960s when there was no global competition, but it is not okay now. Senior executives and their managers need to realize that, if they manage by the numbers, they will fail. There is a new paradigm of business in the current global economies, and we must change our approach to everything. Tom Johnson, professor of cost management at the School of Business Management, Portland State University, has pointed out that "business performance would improve dramatically if top management eliminated all existing management accounting control systems and started people talking about customer satisfaction being everyone's job" (Johnson 1992). This is truly a revolution.

A War Story about Budgets

I was at one time an inventory manager for spare parts for Rank Xerox in Europe. I was responsible for 13 countries and 27 warehouse locations. The management accountants set inventory budgets for each country for each month, and I was expected to meet those budgets.

What would you do if, at the end of the month, you were overstocked in Denmark and understocked in Sweden? You would move material from Denmark to Sweden. The Xerox cost-accounting system was set up so that interplant transfers were deemed to have arrived when the transfer documentation was raised. So I did not have to physically move inventory. I and my first-line supervisors spent a few days each month raising fictitious transfer orders to keep the inventory levels in line with the budget.

Was this good use of our time? Did this serve the customer or improve quality? Did we even think about it? No. It was just a part of playing the game.

Do similar things happen in your company?

Stage 4

Finally, Stage 4 encompasses the following tasks:

- Eliminate traditional cost accounting
- Eliminate inventory tracking
- Eliminate the accounts-payable three-way match
- Use electronic funds transfer

Eliminate Traditional Cost Accounting

Up to now, we have considered the simplification of the cost-accounting system. We will now go one step further. If nonfinancial performance measures are implemented, then the production plant and warehouse can be effectively controlled without any cost accounting at all. We can calculate the average unit cost of production by dividing the total costs by the number of units produced. This will give a broad picture of production efficiency improvement. The cost-accounting systems themselves are no longer required and are, in fact, wasteful and misleading. The financial accounts give all the information required to control the business financially, and the performance measurement reports control the daily running and improvement of the processes and customer service.

Inventory valuation can either be established annually because the process is under control and there is very little variation, or it can be counted as required.

There may still be a need for some inventory transactions because the materials planning systems need to know the stock level of each item and match that against future planned requirements. These transactions are minimized. All transactions are waste and open to error. Fail-safe features like bar-coding standard labels or standard containers are used to eliminate error.

Eliminate Inventory Tracking

Most companies require detailed tracking of their inventory's raw materials, work in process, finished goods, and excess/obsolete materials. The reason for this detailed tracking is that they have too much inventory and it is out of control. This is evidenced by the constant shortages and stock adjustments,* as well as the huge warehouses of aging storage containers.

Lean companies do not focus on *reducing* inventory; in contrast, they focus on *eliminating the causes* of high inventory. As the causes of high inventory are gradually eliminated and the inventory comes under good

---

* It is a curious but widespread paradox that the more inventory you have, the more shortages you have. This is universally true. The reason is that companies with very high inventories have poor control of the inventory, despite their fancy ERP (enterprise resource planning) and warehouse management systems. In order to reduce inventories permanently, it is necessary to bring them under control. When the inventory is brought under control, the complex systems are no longer necessary.

control, then it is no longer necessary to track the materials on the computer systems. The primary methods used to bring inventory under control are pull systems, visual management, and reliable local suppliers:

- *Pull systems* mean that you only move the materials when they are needed and you replenish what you use. These are typically run using kanban cards, pulling relatively low quantities on a frequent basis.
- *Visual management* means that the inventory control and replenishment is done by people going to the stocking location (often called a supermarket) and seeing what is needed. There is no need for complex computer-based inventory systems when the materials are clearly laid out and visually controlled.
- *Reliable local suppliers* means that we work with suppliers that have a consistent track record of perfect quality, correct quantities, and on-time delivery. These attributes—together with the short delivery distance—enable us to pull small quantities frequently and keep our inventory very low.

Once these things are in place, it is no longer necessary to track the inventory on the computer systems. We can eliminate the millions of transactions required to receive the inventory, report the "put away," issue materials, report scrap, count cycles, make adjustments, etc.—to say nothing of the reports and meetings that stem from these totally wasteful processes.

It is unusual for a lean company to completely eliminate its inventory-tracking systems. There are inevitably problem parts numbers or a critical supplier that is not local. But if 60%, 70%, or 80% of the wasteful inventory tracking is removed, a great deal has been gained. And the inventory is under better control, leading to (almost) no shortages, smoother production, no expediting, and better service to the customers.

Similarly, as pull systems and visual management are introduced into the production and distribution processes, there is no longer any need for inventory tracking and control throughout the production process or finished-goods warehouses. It is common for lean companies to have finished-goods supermarkets—particularly for their fast-moving items—and these are used to provide level schedules in production when customer demand is fluctuating. The supermarkets pull their replenishment from production using kanban cards, and sales orders are used to pull non-stocked items. These methods, together with short production lead times, provide sufficient control for the company to run very well without the need for complex and wasteful inventory-tracking systems.

Eliminate the Accounts Payable Three-Way Match

The accounts payable three-way match—whereby we match the invoice from the supplier with the receiving transaction and the purchase order to ensure we pay the correct amount for our materials—is another manifestation of the chaos of traditional manufacturing companies. But as the company introduces pull systems and visual management—and as it buys the majority of its requirements from local, certified suppliers—it becomes increasingly unnecessary to go through these AP peregrinations.

Once again, the issue is to eliminate the need for the AP three-way match by eliminating the causes of errors—for example:

- One cause is an error or complexity in the purchase order. We can overcome this by having long-term contracts with the suppliers that clearly specify terms and prices.
- Another cause is a quantity error. We can overcome this by having standard kanban quantities, small quantities, and standard containers. This is similar to an egg carton in a grocery store: it is easy to see if you have your dozen eggs, and it is easy to see if any are broken.
- A third problem is quality: This can be largely overcome by having local certified suppliers whose quality we can trust. This eliminates the need to inspect the materials when they are delivered. If there is an occasional quality problem, this will become apparent very quickly because the low inventory levels mean that the items will be used almost immediately, and the problem will cause production to stop. There will be a small quantity of defective parts because the delivery quantities are small, and the problem can be rectified quickly because the supplier is local.

When these kinds of methods are in place, it becomes easy to work out how much you need to pay the supplier. You pay for what you have received, and the supplier no longer sends you an invoice. When the materials come in, there is a single receiving transaction that is usually achieved from a bar code on the kanban card. This transaction will expense the value of the materials to the value-stream and post the amount to accounts payable. The supplier is then paid according to the terms of the contract.

Use Electronic Funds Transfer

If the accounts payable invoices can be created automatically, it follows logically that payment can be made automatically using electronic funds transfer. If suppliers are required to provide just-in-time deliveries and zero defects, it is only fair that they be given just-in-time payments. Electronic funds transfer, whether automatic or manually driven, saves several transactions. It is no longer necessary to print a check, sign it, and mail it. This saves time and reduces complexity. The supplier receiving the check does not need to enter a cash-receipt transaction, because the computer does that automatically. The transactions are automatic and they are accurate. Once again, the manual transactions are eliminated, and the quality of the information is improved.

SUMMARY

Lean manufacturers do not run their companies "by the numbers." Instead, the concepts of *quality* and *customer service* are paramount. If the company creates high value for the customer and takes care of the detailed process improvement issues, then the financial numbers will take care of themselves.

There is no need for the detailed cost and management accounting procedures that are common in traditional companies. The financial accounting system provides all the information a manager needs to run the company financially, and the nonfinancial performance measures ensure that the production plants, warehouses, and offices are under control and making continuous improvement.

The accounting systems should be systematically simplified as the company implements world-class manufacturing techniques and ideas. Eliminate everything in the accounting systems that is not value-added— which is almost everything. Eliminate transactions: they are wasteful and create error.

Make the accounting systems simple, easy-to-use, visible and understandable, relevant, and flexible.

QUESTIONS

1. What simplification actions can your company take right now?
2. What short-term benefits would be derived from implementing this simplification approach?
3. What obstacles would you encounter when trying to implement accounting simplification?

5

Value-Stream Accounting

Value-stream accounting is one of the cornerstones of accounting in lean companies. We do not collect costs by departments, or products, or individual production jobs. Instead, we collect costs by value-stream—typically, once a week. There are several reasons for this:

- Value-stream cost and revenue information can be gathered quickly and simply. When a company has a well-defined value-stream organization, gathering the costs of the value-stream each week is simple and straightforward.
- The cost information is direct cost, with few or no allocations. This means that the cost information is immediately understandable to the people who need to use it. In contrast, an income statement-developed using traditional standard costing (or its complicated older brothers, like activity-based costing or resource consumption accounting) shows the costs based on complex methods of overhead allocation that render the information meaningless. The inappropriateness of the standard costs is then offset by a list of thoroughly obscure variances. These reports provide very little meaningful information for the people who have to use them.*
- Allocation of costs leads to meaningless information. Allocations lead to meetings! In contrast, if we can provide financial information that is direct and clear, then we are providing meaningful information that people can use with confidence.

---

* In their book, *Real Numbers*, Cunningham and Fiume (2004) state: "The average recipient of a standard cost-based profit and loss statement does not understand the document in his hands. It communicates nothing."

- The financial information is timely—typically, weekly. This means that value-stream managers can use this information to control and reduce their costs. The information on the reports is still "warm" because it reflects recent events. The more frequently information is reported, the better it can be controlled.
- Value-stream cost information is relevant to and actionable by the value-stream managers. The value-stream managers are responsible for the revenues, costs, and profits of the value-stream, and the information on the report is directly relevant to doing their jobs.
- Value-stream accounting gives better information for routine decision making such as quoting, make/buy, capital acquisition, sourcing, etc. The reason for this is that the information provided is real. In contrast, when decisions are made using standard costs (or any other absorption-based product costing method), the information is not real because it includes a lot of allocation assumptions. Value-stream accounting only collects the real costs that have occurred within the value-stream.
- Value-stream accounting focuses attention on the value-streams. Managing by value-stream is one of the five key principles of lean thinking.* Value-stream accounting provides the information for the financial management of the value-streams.
- Value-stream accounting fosters and supports value-stream teamwork. The purpose of developing value-stream teams is to create a mini-entrepreneurial company within the company that is focused on growing the business for the products manufactured within the value-stream.† Weekly value-stream income statements assist in this team-based endeavor.
- The cost and revenue information can be collected using very few transactions. The financial information is a summary of the direct costs of the value-stream for a week. There is no need for detailed and complicated, transaction-based systems common in traditional manufacturing companies.

---

* The five principles are (1) focus on customer value, (2) manage by value-stream, (3) maximize flow at the customer pull, (4) empower your people, (5) pursue perfection (Maskell and Baggaley 2004; Jones and Womack 1996).
† The job description for a value-stream manager is to (1) grow the business, (2) create more value for the customers, (3) eliminate waste in every process, and (4) make tons of money.

HOW DOES VALUE-STREAM ACCOUNTING WORK?

Value-stream costs are collected as the direct costs of the value-stream for the week or month. The direct costs of the value-stream include:

- Labor costs
- Material costs
- Machine costs
- Outside process costs
- Facilities costs
- Other costs

Let's look at each in a bit more detail.

Labor Costs

Labor costs include the burdened labor costs of all the people who work in the value-stream. This information is readily available from the payroll system in most companies and represents the total direct costs of employing the people. There is no distinction made between the so-called *direct* labor and *indirect* labor: if someone works in the value-stream, his or her costs are included, and it does not matter if that person makes the product, moves materials, is a quality engineer, maintenance worker, or a manager. If they work in the value-stream, their costs are included, as shown in Figure 5.1.

Material Costs

Material costs become increasingly simple to track as the company becomes more lean and as quantities of purchased materials and components remain low and under visual control. The "touchstone" is 30 days or less of purchased inventory, and visual pull systems. When this is in place, then the cost of materials is the same as the purchases.

When a lean company has a pull system with its suppliers, the material used for production triggers a kanban replenishment from the supplier, as shown in Figure 5.2. This results in a kanban quantity delivered from the supplier with a short lead time. What we buy from the supplier is what we

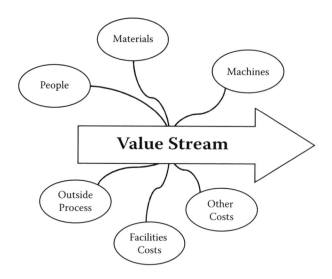

FIGURE 5.1
Types of value-stream cost.

have used. The materials costs come from the receiving transaction. The receiving transaction is set up in the system so that the cost of the materials is debited as a materials cost to the value-stream.

A similar approach can be achieved when the company has large inventories and purchases using manufacturing resource planning (MRPII) or a similar traditional, push system (see Figure 5.3). The system purchases the materials from the supplier using a purchase order. When the materials are used in the value-stream, a kanban card is used to move a kanban quantity

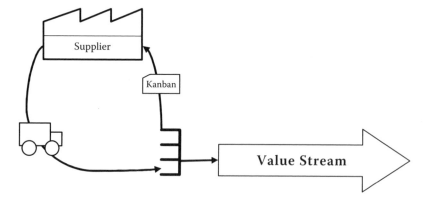

FIGURE 5.2
Materials cost with a pull system.

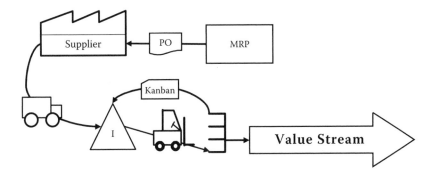

FIGURE 5.3
Materials costs with MRP inventory.

of materials into the value-stream supermarket. The materials costs are expensed to the value-stream at the time of the move from the warehouse to the supermarket.

Many lean companies use a combination of both of these approaches. Although the majority of their materials are on kanban-pull, there are some problem parts that are handled more traditionally because their supply is not under good control.

Machine Costs

Machine costs usually consist of depreciation. Although this is not a real cash cost, most companies find it helpful to have the machine costs reflected in the value-stream statements. Some companies use replacement cost as the basis for the depreciation, particularly when they have similar value-streams using new and older equipment, and they do not want one to appear higher or lower in cost than the other.

Companies with heavy utility costs often report those costs against the machines. The rule of thumb is that if the utility costs are important enough to differentiate by machine, then the usage of utilities should be metered and reported as direct costs. If not, then the utility costs are usually included in facilities costs.

Some companies report their spare parts against the machine costs, whereas most companies will report them as "other" costs. This choice is made according to the materiality and controllability of these costs.

Outside Process Costs

Outside process costs are tracked visually. Many companies have the problem that the invoices for the outside processes come too late to provide valid cost reporting on the value-stream income statement. Lean companies handle these issues visually.

A visual board is placed at the shipping dock where the items are shipped to the outside process companies. Every outside process supplier has a long-term contract with the company defining the jobs they do, together with the technical information, lead-times, pricing, terms, and so forth. When a job is shipped out, the authorizing document is a kanban, and a copy of the kanban is posted on the visual board to show that the job has been shipped out. When a job is received back into the plant, the kanban relating to it on the board is turned over: often, the back of the kanban is a different color. At the end of the week, the person in the value-stream responsible for the control of outside processes can easily count how many jobs have been completed this week and calculate their cost. Figure 5.4 provides an example of a value-stream income statement.

In addition to this, there may be a transaction when the outside process job is received that posts the cost of the job to the value-stream and vouchers the accounts payable account for the supplier. This would maintain a good record of the outside process costs, and it eliminates the need for the contractor to provide an invoice. Payments are made based on the subcontract jobs received, and an invoice is unnecessary.

REVENUES		
Sales	$32,332	
Adjustments	($162)	
NET SALES	$32,170	
VARIABLE COSTS	$10,116	
CONTRIBUTION	$22,054	69%
LABOR	$11,084	34%
MACHINES	$583	2%
OUTSIDE PROCESS	$1,154	4%
FACILITIES	$247	1%
OTHER	$2,334	7%
TOTAL COSTS	$15,402	48%
OPERATING PROFIT	$6,652	21%

FIGURE 5.4
Example of a value-stream income statement.

Facilities Costs

Facilities costs are allocated based on square footage (or square meters). We try to avoid allocations because they cause confusion and meetings, but in the case of facilities costs, we want to provide a tangible incentive for the value-stream managers to use less space, so we charge them "rent" for the space they use. The only difference from traditional facilities allocation is that we charge the value-stream manager only for the space he or she uses. There will be a good deal of space within the organization that is not charged to any value-stream and is assigned to a support cost category. This avoids the problem where the value-stream uses less space only to find that the cost per foot has increased—and the company is no better off.

Other Costs

Other costs of the value-stream include spare parts, supplies, consumable tools, travel, and so forth. It is common for someone in the value-stream to be responsible for buying these items. They are mostly purchased from suppliers that have long-term contracts and are paid for by credit card (or purchase card). The responsible person keeps track of what he or she has spent and reports it weekly.

The income statement is created by showing the sales made for the product manufactured in the value-stream that week, the costs, and the profitability of the value-stream. An example is shown in Figure 5.5.

PLAIN-ENGLISH INCOME STATEMENTS

One objective of the value-stream income statements is to present them in "plain English."[*] The income statements are largely cash based and show the financial information in a way that is straightforward and clear. Anyone in the company would be able to understand these income statements and use them for controlling costs, reducing costs, and making decisions. They involve none of the opaque accounting methods like

---

[*] Cunningham and Fiume (2004).

MACHINES VALUE STREAM			Week: October 23	
REVENUES				
Sales	$32,332		$32,332	
Adjustments	($162)		($162)	
NET SALES	$32,170		$32,170	
VARIABLE COSTS			$10,116	
Materials	$7,853		$7,853	24%
Commissions	$2,263		$2,263	7%
CONTRIBUTION	$22,054		$22,054	69%
	PRODUCTION	**SUPPORT**		
LABOR	$8,320	$2,763	$11,084	34%
Labor Cost	$5,778	$2,142		
Fringes	$2,542	$621		
MACHINES	$380	$203	$583	2%
Machines	$380	$85		
Rentals		$118		
OUTSIDE PROCESS	$1,072	$82	$1,154	4%
FACILITIES	$247		$247	1%
OTHER	$1,459	$875	$2,334	7%
Supplies	$470	$131		
Tooling	$521			
Scrap	$371			
Warranty	$97			
Professional		$69		
Travel		$158		
Advertising		$87		
Recruitment		$28		
Miscellaneous		$402		
TOTAL COSTS	$11,478	$3,923	$15,402	48%
OPERATING PROFIT			$6,652	21%

FIGURE 5.5
Detailed value-stream income statement.

standard costs, variances, or absorption. When people are given the right information, they will make the right decisions and use the information in positive ways. This kind of financial report moves people to do lean work, whereas a traditional statement will motivate non-lean activities.

Closing the Books

If we have weekly income statements for controlling costs, reducing costs, and managing the value-stream, can we also use the same approach to provide monthly financial reporting? The answer, of course, is "yes." The financial information can be gathered for each value-stream for the whole month, and it can be consolidated with the financial information for the other value-streams. This way, we have a single accounting system that is used for both *management* accounting *within* the company and *financial* accounting for *external* reporting.

	MACHINES	ACCESSORIES	SPARES	NEW PRODUCTS	SALES & MARKETING	SUPPORT	TOTAL COMPANY
REVENUE							
Sales							
Adjustments							
NET SALES							
VARIABLE COSTS							
CONTRIBUTION							
LABOR							
MACHINES							
OUTSIDE PROCESS							
FACILITIES							
OTHER							
TOTAL COSTS							
OPERATING PROFIT							

Inventory Change		
Corporate Overhead		
Exchange Rate Adjustment		
NET PROFIT		

FIGURE 5.6
Consolidated income statement.

For example, the company whose income statement is shown in Figure 5.6 has three order-fulfillment value-streams, a new product development value-stream, and a sales and marketing value-stream. The "sales and marketing" value-stream is shown in quotes because it is not theoretically correct to have a sales aand marketing value-stream. The sales and marketing processes should all be a part of one of the order fulfillment or the new product development value-streams, but it is quite common to designate a sales and marketing value-stream because these processes are often organized very differently from the order fulfillment or product development value-streams. This is not theoretically correct, but it is pragmatic and can work well.

In addition to these value-streams, there is also a "support" column. This contains the costs of people and departments that are not in any value-stream. These support costs must be small and will consist of people like the plant manager or general manager, financial accounting, human resources, sometimes IT (information technology), and other departments that support the value-streams but are not an integral part of the value-stream.

To calculate the company-wide month-end statement, all we need to do is to add across the financial information to create a consolidated income statement. In the example shown in Figure 5.6, the company made $97,334 profit this month, which is a return of 17% on sales. This is not the end of the story, however. There are a few adjustments that need to be made to make the statement suitable for external reporting. If inventory levels have increased or decreased during the month, there will be an impact on company profitability.

There are also other "external" costs that may be applied to the operations. In the example in Figure 5.6, the company is required to pay $8,576 to cover the overheads of the corporation beyond the plant. There is also an adjustment to the bottom-line profit caused by changes in international exchange rates. These adjustments are never applied to the value-streams because they are not relevant to the value-streams. The company is run using the numbers above the line, and the below-the-line adjustments are used merely to bring the statement in line with external reporting.

When these adjustments are complete, the statement can be used for any kind of external reporting because it is fully compliant with GAAP (generally accepted accounting principles), SEC requirements, IRS requirements, and IAS (International Accounting Standards).

"Our Corporate People Need the Traditional Statement"

There is often, particularly in large multinational companies, a need to continue to create the traditional financial statements even though a division is using the plain-English or lean statements. There is no need to run any parallel systems to do this. The traditional statements can be readily re-created from the lean statements with only four or five journal entries. There is usually a need to re-create the variances and to hide the inventory changes in the absorption. But these adjustments can be completed in a few minutes by the controller, and the traditional statement is made available to the corporate people. There is no need for anyone in the company to see these traditional statements as they will cause confusion, but if the bosses want to see the old stuff, let them have it.

Box Score: The Income Statement Is Not Enough

The income statement only shows the financial information about the value-stream. This does not give a good enough understanding of the value-stream performance. Therefore, we need to create a box score. The box score contains three pieces of information:

1. A summary of the value-stream performance measurements
2. A summary of the value-stream income statement
3. A breakdown of how the resources within the value-stream are used, i.e., how much of our valuable resources (primarily people and equipment) is used productively, how much is used nonproductively, and how much available capacity has been freed up within the value-stream

More importantly, we need to see how this three-dimensional view of the value-stream is changing over time as we make more and more strides with lean manufacturing and other lean improvements.

Figure 5.7 shows a box score for the same value-stream as the previous income statement example shown in Figure 5.6. The top sections show the five primary performance measurements used by the value-stream team to monitor the value-stream's performance and drive continuous improvement. The financial information in the lower section is a summary of the income statement shown in Figure 5.5. The section in the middle of the box score shows the capacity usage for the employees within the value-stream and the machines used in the value-stream production cells.

The far right column shows the "goal" for the value-stream. This represents the value-stream box score results based on the implementation of all the lean changes designed into the future-state value-stream map. In other words, this is the expected performance of the value-stream after we have completed the current round of improvement projects. As you can see, the plan is to eliminate waste from the value-stream, and this will free up capacity and enable the value-stream to make and sell more product with the same resources. This is a classic lean growth strategy.

The box score is widely used in value-stream accounting, not only for weekly reporting. It is also used in the following ways:

- For decision making, to show the impacts of various choices on the value-stream
- For capital equipment, to show the impacts of alternative methods and equipment on the value-stream
- In quoting, to understand the profitability, performance measurements, and capacity changes for a proposed quote
- For assessing the financial impact of lean improvement

	Measurement	Owner	2-Oct	9-Oct	16-Oct	23-Oct	30-Oct	23-Jun	30-Jun	GOAL
PERFORMANCE MEASUREMENTS	Productivity Sales/Person	John	$114,575	$111,266	$104,844	$99,349				$128,676
	On-Time Shipment Cust. Request	Wayne	84%	85%	94%	95%				96%
	Dock-to-Dock Time Flow Days	Maria	36	37	32	26				22
	First Pass Yield FTT%	Olivier	82%	82%	82%	84%				85%
	Average Cost per Unit Shipped	Jane	$71	$73	$75	$79				$68
PEOPLE CAPACITY	Productive	Alun & Sabrina	62%	62%	62%	62%				70%
	Non-Productive	Alun & Sabrina	19%	19%	19%	9%				9%
	Available Capacity		19%	19%	19%	29%				21%
MACHINE CAPACITY	Productive	Alun & Sabrina	45%	45%	45%	45%				51%
	Non-Productive	Alun & Sabrina	22%	22%	22%	20%				23%
	Available Capacity		33%	33%	33%	35%				27%
FINANCIAL	REVENUE	John	$155,822	$151,322	$142,588	$135,114				$175,0000
	MATERIALS	Jane	$50,167	$48,718	$45,906	$43,500				$53,524
	CONVERSION	Jane	$63,924	$63,499	$61,287	$62,020				$69,200
	TOTAL COSTS	Jane	$114,091	$112,217	$107,193	$105,520				$122,724
	PROFIT	John	$41,731	$39,105	$35,395	$29,594				$52,276
	RETURN	John	27%	26%	25%	22%				30%

FIGURE 5.7

Box score showing value-stream performance.

FINANCIAL BENEFITS OF LEAN IMPROVEMENT

There is usually an emphasis on cost savings when a company embarks on lean improvement, and cost reduction is an important aim for a lean organization. However, it is quite common in the early stages of lean change to note modest cost savings, even though a great deal of improvement has been achieved within the value-stream. The purpose of lean improvement is to eliminate waste. Very often, this waste elimination does not turn into short-term cost savings. We eliminate waste, and it turns into available capacity. We have reduced the amount of work and machine time—for example, throughout the value-stream—but we still have the same number of people and machines that we had to start with. The gain is that these people and machines have additional capacity that we can use. The financial benefit coming from the lean improvements is determined by what is done with the newly available capacity.

There are three broad categories of choices for newly freed-up capacity, and many variations within each category. We can either:

Make and sell more products to increase the revenues
Use the people and the machines elsewhere
Lay off the people and sell the machines to reduce the costs

The third choice is the traditional way of thinking about productivity improvements and cost reduction, but this choice is not open to a lean organization. A lean organization empowers the value-stream team to make improvement, create more value for the customers, and grow the business. If you "empower" the people and then lay them off every time they make an improvement, the lean process will be short-lived. People are not going to work on improvement projects that cause them (or their buddies) to be "let go." Traditional companies could get away with this cynical strategy because all improvement projects are developed from the top down and implemented by middle managers, but lean companies do not work that way. In contrast, they empower the workforce at every level of the organization. This is the genius of lean thinking: it engages all the people, all the time, with all their skills to create more value for the customer and to eliminate waste.

The first choice is, of course, the best: grow the business by selling more products without increasing any of the production costs except materials. Better yet would be to fill the newly available capacity with products that command a higher price in the market by creating more value than the traditional products. It is vitally important that sales, marketing, and product development be actively involved in the decisions related to lean manufacturing improvements because they are the people who will need to achieve new sales of higher-priced products. Yet it is surprising that many companies think of lean as if it were a shop-floor project! Lean improvement turns waste into available capacity. The financial benefit comes from strategically using this newly available capacity in the most advantageous way, and this needs to be planned in advance.

When the value-stream teams create current-state and future-state value-stream maps, they develop box scores. This shows them the impact of the planned changes on the value-stream's operational performance, capacity usage, and financial outcomes. It is at this point—before any kaizens have been planned or completed—that the company must decide how it will benefit financially from the changes. A strategy needs to be set for sales growth, new-product introduction, and other activities that will use the capacity to its advantage.

In the example in Figure 5.8, the current state shows a well-balanced value-stream: 62% of the people's time is spent making the product and less than 20% of their time is available capacity. The rule of thumb for a value-stream is that 15%–20% available capacity is required to run an effective process. We are not trying to fill all capacity because there needs to be spare capacity to cope with demand variability and the inevitable disruptions and problems.

If the people introduce the changes set out in the future-state map, they will free up 10% more available capacity. Working with the sales and marketing people, a plan is put in place to increase sales and fill this capacity. The sales people can only commit to an 8% increase over the three-month period between the current- and future-state maps, and that is the amount put into the plan.

Often, these discussions are iterative. The sales and marketing people work together with the production and purchasing people within the value-stream to develop an improvement program that will create the right amount of capacity in the right places within the value-stream to maximize the impact for the company. This cross-functional cooperative

			CURRENT	LAYOFFS	SELL MORE PRODUCT	NEW HIGHER PRICED PRODUCTS
PERFORMANCE MEASUREMENTS	Productivity Sales/Person	John	$114,575	$127,723	$128,676	$132,202
	On-Time Shipment Cust. Request	Wayne	84%	85%	94%	94%
	Dock-to-Dock Time Flow Days	Maria	36	25	22	22
	First Pass Yield FTT %	Olivier	82%	83%	86%	86%
	Average Cost per Unit Shipped	Jane	$71	$67	$68	$69
PEOPLE CAPACITY	Productive	Alun & Sabrina	62%	70%	70%	62%
	Non-Productive		19%	9%	9%	9%
	Available Capacity		19%	21%	21%	29%
MACHINE CAPACITY	Productive	Alun & Sabrina	45%	55%	51%	51%
	Non-Productive		22%	20%	23%	23%
	Available Capacity		33%	25%	26%	26%
FINANCIAL	REVENUE	John	$155,822	$155,822	$175,000	$179,795
	MATERIALS	Jane	$50,167	$45,717	$53,524	$54,059
	CONVERSION	Jane	$63,924	$61,185	$69,200	$70,366
	TOTAL COSTS	Jane	$114,091	$106,902	$122,724	$124,425
	PROFIT	John	$41,731	$48,920	$52,276	$55,369
	RETURN	John	27%	31%	30%	31%

FIGURE 5.8
Box score showing alternative uses of capacity.

effort is a very important aspect of lean thinking and lean culture. In lean, we always "work by the numbers." That is, we calculate the impact of the future-state plans, we analyze the opportunities, and we decide the most beneficial route forward. This is lean thinking.

Another Way to Look at the Potential Benefits of Lean Change

When we have a good understanding of how the value-stream's resources are used (i.e., how much is used productively, how much is used nonproductively, and how much is available capacity), then we can calculate how much money is spent wastefully. Only the productive capacity is adding any value; the rest is waste. Although it may not be possible to eliminate all of the waste, this analysis shows the potential profitability of the value-stream as, over time, the value-stream team relentlessly removes the waste and creates more value. This is illustrated in Figure 5.9.

Decision Making without a Standard Cost: A Case Study

For the most part, within lean accounting, we do not recommend the calculation of a product cost. Any method of product cost calculation makes assumptions about the variability of the costs that are not true when making decisions.* For example:

- *Standard costing* assumes that all costs are variable: material costs, labor costs, and overhead costs that are usually applied as a percentage of labor cost.
- *Activity-based costing* works the same way, but it applies the overheads in more complicated ways.

	PRODUCTIVE	NON-PRODUCTIVE	AVAILABLE CAPACITY	TOTAL
REVENUES				
Sales	$135,794			$135,794
Adjustments	($630)			($630)
NET SALES	$135,114			$135,114
VARIABLE COSTS$	$43,500	$0	$0	$43,500
CONTRIBUTION	$91,614	$0	$0	$91,614
LABOR	$27,350	$8,381	$8,381	$44,112
MACHINES	$1,101	$538	$808	$2,447
OUTSIDE PROCESS$	$4,385	$0	$0	$4,385
FACILITIES	$643	$197	$197	$1,037
OTHER	$6,222	$1,907	$1,907	$10,036
TOTAL COSTS$	$39,702	$11,024	$11,293	$62,018
	64%	18%	18%	100%
NET PROFIT	$51,913	($11,024)	($11,293)	$29,596
RETURN	38%			22%

FIGURE 5.9
Income statement showing the cost of waste.

---

* One of the foremost pioneers of standard costing methods, Alexander H. Church, recognized the limitations of standard cost accounting with regard to decision making and pricing. He is particularly concerned about the variability of the costs. "Now the cost of selling has not any proportionate relation to cost of making at all. And the real difficulty of basing the incidence of general charges on shop cost is that these charges do not get higher in the majority of cases.… It is not often that the price obtained for an article is otherwise than ruled by the state of the market" (Church 1908, 124).

- Companies focusing on material contribution alone assume that no costs are variable other than materials. It is a mistake to try to make decisions using a calculated product cost.

The routine decisions relating to quoting, profitability, make/buy, sourcing, product "rationalization," and so forth are best made by looking at the impact on the value-stream as a whole, rather than the individual product. The value-stream statements will give you accurate information about what will happen financially as you make changes to revenues, material costs, employee costs, machine costs, and other operations costs. And this information is calculated in simple and understandable ways.

In reality, many companies do not rely entirely on the standard costs when making these kinds of decisions. They often have other methods that they bring out and use when they need to understand a sourcing issue, for example. In lean accounting, we are advocating the use of these simple, straightforward methods that give accurate information instead of having a series of informal approaches.

In the example shown in Figure 5.10, a customer has requested a quote (RFQ) for 500 items per month over the next 12 months, and has set a target price of $80 per unit. The standard cost for the item is $75, and the company requires a minimum of a 15% margin. The target price of $80 only yields a 6.25% margin and the company decided to "no quote" on the RFQ.

The sales manager was unhappy about the outcome and asked the purchasing manager to see if the product could be purchased from a low-cost country at a reasonable price. Sure enough, the item can be sourced in a low-cost country for only $40. The company recognizes that there are additional costs associated with low-cost-country sourcing and adds an additional 7.5% overhead costs to all of these purchases. This brings the landed cost to $43 and provides a 46% margin on the sale.

The purchasing manager was about to write a contract with the Chinese supplier to purchase 6,000 units to cover the customer's annual needs when the value-stream manager looked at the possibility of making the product in-house rather than outsourcing it. The value-stream did not have enough capacity to manufacture the product, but hiring a few more people and purchasing a new machine would provide the additional capacity required. The additional costs to purchase the raw materials and obtain the extra capacity came to $32,148 per month.

The outcomes are shown in the box score in Figure 5.10:

		CURRENT	STANDARD COST	OUTSOURCE TO CHINA	MAKE IN HOUSE
PERFORMANCE MEASUREMENTS	Productivity — John	$114,575	$114,575	$143,987	$143,987
	On-Time Shipment — Wayne	84%	84%	78%	84%
	Dock-to-Dock Time — Maria	36	36	48	32
	First Pass Yield — Olivier	82%	82%	75%	82%
	Average Cost — Jane	$71	$71	$71	$70
PEOPLE CAPACITY	Productive	62%	62%	62%	73%
	Non-Productive — Alun & Sabrina	19%	19%	19%	20%
	Available Capacity	19%	19%	19%	7%
MACHINE CAPACITY	Productive	45%	45%	45%	48%
	Non-Productive — Alun & Sabrina	22%	22%	22%	21%
	Available Capacity	33%	33%	33%	31%
FINANCIAL	REVENUE — John	$155,822	$155,822	$195,822	$196,822
	MATERIALS — Jane	$50,167	$50,167	$84,545	$75,923
	CONVERSION — Jane	$63,924	$63,924	$63,924	$70,316
	TOTAL COSTS — Jane	$114,091	$114,091	$148,469	$146,239
	PROFIT — John	$41,731	$41,731	$47,353	$49,583
	RETURN — John	27%	27%	24%	25%

FIGURE 5.10
Box score used for make/buy decision.

- Column 3 shows the current-state box score information for the value-stream.
- Column 4 shows the impact of making the decision using a standard cost and margin approach. Column 4 is the same as column 3 because this approach leads to turning down the order.
- Column 5 shows the impact on the value-stream if we decide to buy the product from a low-cost country.
- Column 6 shows the impact on the value-stream if we decide to increase the value-stream capacity and make the product in-house.

There is no clear-cut "right answer" to this decision because, like any business decision, there are a number of other issues to be taken into account. But the box score diagram in Figure 5.10 shows the operational, capacity, and financial impact of each of the three approaches. We do not look at the profitability of the individual product; we take account of the impact of the choices on the value-stream as a whole. The calculation of margin on the individual product does not give us a true understanding of the financial outcomes of the decision. But looking at the *impact on the value-stream as a whole* shows us—in real, reliable numbers—the outcome of each scenario. From this, we can make an appropriate business decision.

A similar approach is used for all routine decisions: quoting, profitability, make/buy, sourcing, product rationalization, capital purchases, etc. The simplistic idea that the standard cost enables you to make these kinds of decisions has done great harm to thousands of companies, and particularly to companies pursuing a lean transformation.

PRODUCT COSTING

In general, we would advocate that there is no need to calculate a product cost for an individual product. The idea of an individual product cost is quite misleading, and it leads to misunderstandings about cost and profitability and to poor decisions. In addition, a standard cost is usually calculated to four or five decimal places, giving an illusion of accuracy to something that is chock-full of false assumptions.

Having said that, there are some occasions when a product cost is needed. For example, some companies need product costs for the purpose of calculating transfer prices between company locations. This is particularly true when the locations are in different countries, because many countries require costs to be shown on the import/export documents.

When a product cost is required, it can be calculated quite simply. The cost of the product is variable cost plus the cost of manufacture. The variable cost usually includes materials or component costs, and the cost of any outside processes. The manufacturing costs derive from the value-stream costing information.

For example, if a value-stream has total conversion costs (excluding the variable costs) of $96,000 per week and there are 80 hours in a week, then the cost per hour is $1,200, or $20 per minute. A product with a cycle time of one minute will have a conversion cost of $20, and a product with a cycle time of two minutes will have a conversion cost of $40. The conversion

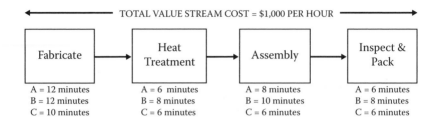

FIGURE 5.11
Product costing based on the rate of flow.

cost of the product is dependent on the product's rate of flow through the value-stream, and it is unrelated to the amount of labor required to make the item. It is the rate of flow—the cycle time*—that determines the conversion costs of a product.

The rate of flow of a product through the value-stream is determined by the slowest step in the process. This is usually referred to as the bottleneck or constraint in the process. The bottleneck process in the example shown in Figure 5.11 is the initial fabrication step. If the process is making Product A only, then five units can be made in one hour, and the conversion cost of Product A is $200 ($1,000 per hour/5 units). Similarly, Product B is constrained to five units per hour, and the conversion cost is also $200, despite the fact that there is more touch labor required to make the B. Product C spends less time in the bottleneck operation—only 10 minutes fabrication—and so six units can be made in one hour. The conversion cost of Product C is thus $167 ($1,000 per hour/6 units). The cost of product is primarily related to rate of flow through the value-stream and not the amount of touch-labor time required to make the product.

Remember: the *price* of a product is not related to the *cost* of the product. The price for a B may be higher than the price for an A. But the cost of the two products is the same.

---

* *Takt time* is the rate of customer demand. If the customers demand is 240 units per day on average, then the takt time is 8 hours × 3600 seconds per hour/240 units = 120 seconds per unit. If our process can produce one unit every 100 seconds, then the *cycle time* is 100 seconds. It may be that six people are required to make the product, and each person performs 100 seconds of work; so the *touch-labor time* is 600 seconds, but the cycle time is still 100 seconds. The *lead time* is touch-labor time plus any waiting or delays in the process, i.e., the amount of time it takes from starting production to completing the product.

To calculate the cost of a product, the features and characteristics method is used. We define the features and characteristics of the product that determines the rate of flow through the bottleneck operation in the value-stream. From this, the conversion cost can be calculated and added to the material costs to obtain the product cost.

The example shown in Figure 5.12 is a features and characteristics cost matrix for a value-stream making plastic seals. The mold process is the bottleneck, and the rate of flow through the molding process is determined by the number of cavities in the molds. Small products have more cavities per mold than the larger products. The cost of the materials is determined by the number of cavities as well as by the type of material, which has different prices and also different scrap and wastage rates.

The combination of the number of mold cavities and the type of material is sufficient to calculate the product costs for any item manufactured in the value-stream. Although the value-stream manufactures hundreds of different products, the cost of those products can be determined from the table shown on the left in Figure 5.12. In reality, a table similar to the one shown on the right in Figure 5.12 is more commonly used. This shows the ratio of the product costs from the average cost of products manufactured, and it enables the current raw material costs to be applied. This means that the product cost can be calculated at any time using the most recent average, value-stream product cost, and the most recent commodity prices.

The features and characteristics method provides a more accurate product cost, and it is (usually) much simpler to calculate and understand. However, this product cost is also wrong and should never be used for decision making or other important tasks. This product cost may be used for valuing inventory when inventory levels are too high or too chaotic to use simpler methods, or when the items are excess or obsolete. This

		MATERIAL			
		EU-12	EU-25	VA-03	VA-25
	5	$2.54	$2.53	$4.85	$12.07
NUMBER OF MOLD CAVITIES	10	$1.27	$1.28	$2.44	$.03
	20	$0.64	$0.63	$1.22	$.02
	30	$0.42	$0.42	$0.81	$.0

		MATERIAL			
		EU-12	EU-25	VA-03	VA-25
	5	23%	23%	44%	110%
NUMBER OF MOLD CAVITIES	10	12%	11%	22%	55%
	20	6%	6%	11%	27%
	30	4%	4%	7%	18%
Material Price		$0.0770	$0.0766	$0.1460	$0.3657

FIGURE 5.12
Features and characteristics cost matrix.

product cost is quite suitable for transfer pricing calculations and other times where standard costs have been traditionally used.

SUMMARY

Lean companies eliminate standard cost accounting in favor of value-stream accounting. The primary collection and reporting of revenues and costs is the value-stream, rather than the product. Income statements are reported for each value-stream, usually weekly, and the value-stream manager has P&L (profit and loss) responsibility for the products flowing through his or her value-stream. In addition to order fulfillment value-streams, the same reporting is used for new product development and sales and marketing value-streams.

Lean organizations also make use of the box score to provide a three-dimensional understanding of value-stream performance. The box score shows the following information:

- The key value-streams' operational performance measurements
- A summary of the financial performance
- A breakdown of how the value-stream's resource capacity is used: productive time, nonproductive time, and available capacity

Box scores are used widely as the lingua franca within the company when addressing the issues related to value-stream performance, decision making, financial benefits of changes, and other needs.

The box score is used to understand the financial and operational impact of lean improvements. When developing a current- and future-state value-stream map, a box score is developed to show (a) the impact of the changes on the value-stream's operational and financial performance and (b) how the capacity usage changes as waste is eliminated from the value-stream processes. This is a simple yet powerful tool for creating a strategy to maximize the financial and operational benefit of lean improvement.

There is no need to calculate a cost for individual items because other methods are used to achieve the tasks currently requiring a standard product cost. These include pricing, make/buy decisions, margins and profitability, performance measurements, capital equipment purchases, inventory valuation, transfer pricing, and so forth. However, when a product is required, the features and characteristics method provides a simple, practical, and valid product cost.

QUESTIONS

1. Does your company have a clear picture of the value-streams within the plant or organization?
2. What would it take in your location to collect data on revenues and cost by value-stream each week, without imposing a burdensome task?
3. Would you foresee a ready acceptance within your company for decision making based on actual financial changes rather than the simplistic and erroneous idea of margins?
4. In what ways would a box score—combining operational measurements, financial results, and resource capacity information—be helpful in your journey to lean transformation?

6

Value-Added Management

It is important to understand the distinction between value-added and non-value-added (VA/NVA) activities. Everything an organization does is a process. The organization may be divided into functional departments for the purposes of management, but the company's processes will often cross those departmental barriers. The purpose of value-added management is to gain an understanding of the processes required to run the business, and then to determine if those processes are administered well.

Two techniques are required:

Process mapping (or value-stream mapping*), which is a graphical method of describing the processes within the company
Value-added analysis, which weighs the activities within a process to determine whether that activity contributes value or merely creates cost

Everything that happens within a company is a process or a series of processes. An organization's success is determined by how well those processes are performed. Most companies think of their activities in terms of the departments doing the jobs, and they fail to understand the underlying cross-functional processes involved.

Lean companies work hard at eliminating departmental divisions. Often, the companies reorganize around their value-streams rather than the departments. The focus changes from the departments to the

---

* Value-stream mapping is a particular kind of process map that is widely used in lean manufacturing. Value-stream maps are designed to map the entire flow for a product family through a production plant and are used to plan improvements to the value-stream (Rother and Shook 1999).

customers (both internal and external). Teams are created to serve the customers through reengineered processes designed to thoroughly meet the customer's needs.

The purpose of process mapping and value-added analysis is to

- Understand these processes
- Determine their strategic importance
- Measure how effectively the processes achieve their objectives

Sometimes, value-added analysis leads to radical restructuring of the company to focus the processes on the customer and eliminate activities and tasks that create cost but do nothing to achieve the company's goals. At other times, it is used to create small but continuous improvement in the company's operations that gradually eliminate waste and improve performance.

The accountant has a vital role to play in this process of radical change and continuous improvement by working as part of the team to accomplish all of the following tasks:

- Map the processes
- Analyze the activities
- Provide cost information about the processes
- Create improvement
- Eliminate cost

WHAT IS A PROCESS?

According to the *American Heritage Dictionary*, a process is a system of operations in the production of something or a series of actions, changes, or functions that bring about an end or result. A process is a series of actions that transform some inputs into an output. The input may be raw material and the output a finished product; or the input may be a product idea and the output a design; or the input may be a sales order and the output an invoice to the customer.

A process is generally initiated by a customer need, and the inputs come from internal or external suppliers (see Figure 6.1). Various mechanisms

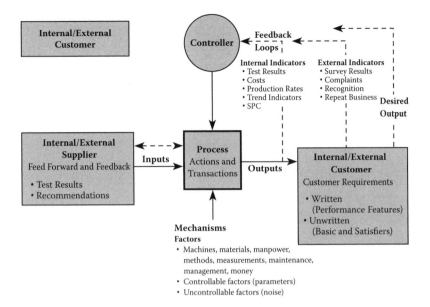

FIGURE 6.1
Elements of a process.

are applied to the inputs to create the output, under the jurisdiction of the process controller or value-stream manager responsible for the process. These mechanisms include the famous eight *M*s:

1. Machines
2. Materials
3. Manpower
4. Methods
5. Measurement
6. Maintenance
7. Management
8. Money

To fully understand a process, it is necessary to know the inputs, the outputs, the controllers, the mechanisms required, and any feedback loops within the process. Simple processes are usually well understood, but the more complex processes, spanning several departments or areas within the company, require detailed analysis.

VALUE-ADDED ANALYSIS

Value-added analysis assumes that a process consists of two different elements:

Value-added activities directly contribute to serving the customer and add value in the eyes of the customer

Non-value-added activities create cost without adding to value of the product or service

A simple example of this is shown in Figure 6.2. A production process consists of several tasks, including:

• Planning the job
• Moving material
• Waiting for the machine or work center to be available
• Setting up the machine
• Performing the production process
• Moving the finished item
• Inspection

Of all these activities, only the production process time is value-added time. All the other activities are wasteful and do not add any value.

Studies have shown that within an "average" Western production plant, less than 5% of time is spent on value-added activities, and more than 95% of the company's time and effort is spent on activities that create cost without creating any value for the customers. Therefore, a company that spends a considerable amount of time trying to improve the value-added

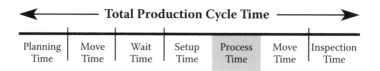

Only the Process Time is Value-Added

FIGURE 6.2
Value-added analysis of a production process.

aspects of its business by concentrating on shop-floor productivity improvements, rather than by concentrating on the elimination of non-value-added activity, will actually *reduce* its value-added percentage. The overall effect of this is marginal improvement. In contrast, a lean company concentrates on eliminating non-value-added activities and creates radical improvement.

Definitions of Value-Added Activities

Simply dividing the activities into value-added and non-value-added can be discouraging to a company or a group of people. It is depressing for an accounting department, for example, to be told that everything it does is non-value-added.

The purpose of value-added analysis is to provide a rational way of understanding the company's processes so that they can be improved and the waste eliminated. This cannot be achieved if the analysis causes people to become discouraged and fearful for their long-term employment prospects.

A better approach is to provide four categories of activities:

1. *Value-added activity* "transforms or shapes a product or service toward that which satisfies the customer's real or perceived wants and needs." Other definitions of a value-added activity are activities that add value to the product from the customer's point of view, or activities that the customers would be prepared to pay for. Examples of value-added activities are:
   - Making the product
   - Performing the service to the customer
   - Sales activities
2. *Strategic activity* indirectly transforms or shapes a product or service and is strategically important to the long-term well-being of the business. Examples of strategic activities are:
   - New product design
   - Training people
   - Marketing
3. *Support activity* does not add value as perceived by the customer but provides a service that maintains the operations process or is driven by actions outside the control of the organization. In other words,

there are non-value-added activities that are essential to support the value-added activities.

4. *Waste* is an activity within the control of the organization that consumes time, resources, or space but does not contribute to the transformation or shaping of the product or service. A wide range of activities fall into the category of waste. These include

- Inspection
- Scrap
- Expediting
- Countless other common activities within manufacturing, distribution, and service organizations

---

VALUE-ADDED ACTIVITY

An activity that transforms or shapes a product or service toward that which satisfies the customer's real and perceived wants and needs

STRATEGIC ACTIVITY

An activity that indirectly transforms or shapes a product or services and is strategically important to the long-term growth of the business

SUPPORT ACTIVITY

An activity that does not add value as perceived by the customers but provides a service that maintains the operation's natural process or is driven by actions outside of the organization's control

CONTROLLABLE WASTE

An activity that is within the control of the organization and consumes time, resources, or space but does not contribute to the transformation or shaping of the product or service

---

Uses of Value-Added Analysis

Value-added analysis is used extensively in lean organizations. Initially, the activities are broken down into their VA/NVA classifications so that potential cost-reduction opportunities can be identified. Later in the analysis, these activities may be broken down further into subactivities or tasks, and each of these will then be classified separately. This way, it is possible to see the non-value-added elements of an activity that is primarily value-added.

An understanding of which activities and tasks are value-added and which are not enables the improvement team to focus on areas of improvement opportunity. Non-value-added activities are to be eliminated; value-added activities are to be improved. Improving a value-added activity includes eliminating the non-value-added elements which may be specific tasks or wasteful elements. These wasteful elements include such things as delays, moving materials, setup or changeover tasks, manufacturing excess inventory, and so on.

A typical value-added analysis is shown in Table 6.1.

PROCESS MAPPING

There are four primary purposes of process mapping:

Knowledge integration
Communication
Analysis
Improvement

A business process crosses departmental barriers within a company, and each segment of the process is the responsibility of different people within the organization. To create an accurate map of this process requires input from each of the people involved. This integration of knowledge across the company makes process mapping a powerful method for truly understanding the company's activities. Frequently, the people involved in process mapping are astonished at the complexity of the final process by the time they have completed the mapping exercise.

TABLE 6.1
Value-Added Analysis for a Production Area

Activity	Cost ($)	Value-Added		Non-Value-Added		Percentage (%)
		Value-Added	Strategic	Support	Waste	
Direct labor	982,440	982,440				54.4%
Dry press fixed costs	67,491	67,491				3.7%
Dry press variable costs	183,112	183,112				10.1%
Supervision/administrative	62,858				62,858	3.5%
Rework	43,132				43,132	2.4%
Scheduling	58,257			58,257		3.22%
Engineering and process improvement	12,699		12,699			0.7%
Emergency maintenance	94,959				94,959	5.26%
Preventive maintenance	121,912			121,912		6.75%
Facilities maintenance	38,625			38,625		2.1%
Ordering direct materials	9,579			9,579		0.5%
Setups and changeovers	36,211				36,211	2.0%
Cleaning lending machines	24,141				24,141	1.3%
Inspection and QA tests	27,463				27,463	1.5%
Rejects	41,668				41,668	2.3%
Total ($)	**1,804,547**	**1,233,043**	**12,699**	**228,373**	**330,432**	
Percentage (%)	100%	68%	1%	13%	18%	

Any team of people working together to create improvement within their organization needs to have a common understanding of the current business process or processes they are dealing with. Process mapping provides an excellent method of communicating the current processes within the team, and at a later stage effectively communicates the changes required to people outside the team who are affected by the changes. A well drawn and well thought out process map provides a much better method of communication than a written procedure.

Process mapping provides a standard method of depicting a process in a logical manner. This lends itself to the analysis of the process. This analysis includes not only accounting issues like the cumulation of costs and value-added analysis, but also the analysis of such issues as cycle time and quality. Process mapping provides a graphical representation of the process; qualitative and quantitative analysis information can be shown on the maps.

The use of maps for the development of process improvements has become a cornerstone of lean improvement methods. A team-based approach to process improvement requires a method that provides a common understanding of the processes and a method to brainstorm the improvement of the process.

Basic Method of Process Mapping

There are many methods for process mapping, and it is not important which particular format is used, provided that there is a clear understanding of the meaning of the symbols and the standards employed. In some cases, it is important to choose a particular style of process map that lends itself to the kind of process improvement task the team is working on, but generally, the style is not significant.

All process mapping techniques use a standard set of symbols to represent the flow of work through a business process. These processes may be physical production processes, administrative processes involving the movement of documents, or logical processes performed by computers and people. A simple and common set of symbols is given in Figure 6.3, and examples of process maps using these symbols are shown in Figures 6.4 and 6.5.

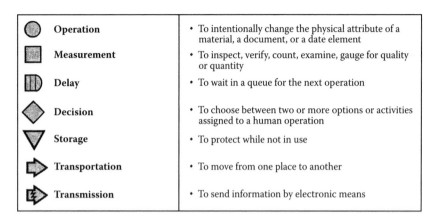

Operation	• To intentionally change the physical attribute of a material, a document, or a date element
Measurement	• To inspect, verify, count, examine, gauge for quality or quantity
Delay	• To wait in a queue for the next operation
Decision	• To choose between two or more options or activities assigned to a human operation
Storage	• To protect while not in use
Transportation	• To move from one place to another
Transmission	• To send information by electronic means

FIGURE 6.3
Process mapping symbols.

Basic Steps to Process Mapping

The first step in process mapping is to define the scope of the project. At first sight, this may seem obvious and easy. In practice, it is often quite difficult to determine the starting point and the stopping point of a process, and it is important that this be decided on by the group of people working on the process.

The second step is to define the boundaries of the process, determine the inputs and outputs, and from this, define the first step and the last step of the process.

The third step is to brainstorm within the group the activities and tasks that take place within the process. It is not necessary to try to move through the process logically at this stage. Brainstorming the tasks and putting them up on the storyboard is all that is required. The best way to do this is to write the tasks and activities on Post-It notes or 3 × 5 cards and then stick them or pin them to a large piece of paper.

Once this is complete, then the team brings the tasks and activities into a logical sequence. It is useful to group the tasks into major activities and then to provide the links and sequence of the process map. This step can take considerable time because the people involved with development of the process map will often have different views of the same process, and time will be needed for these people to talk through their various understandings and arrive at a consensus. Often, additional analysis and information gathering may be required before this consensus can be reached.

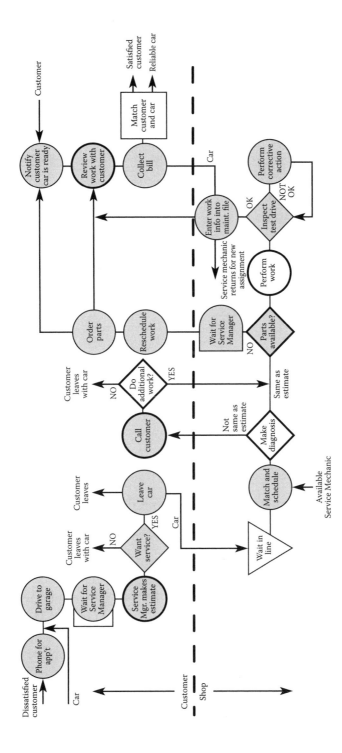

FIGURE 6.4
Process map for servicing a car.

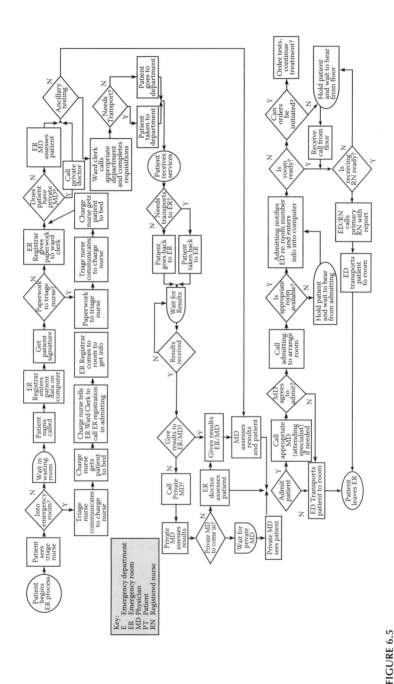

FIGURE 6.5

Process map of a hospital emergency room.

The last step is to draw the final version of the process map and review it with the other people in the company who are involved in this process so that they can validate the accuracy of the map.

The primary purpose of process mapping is for the team to gain an understanding of the processes they are studying and improving, and to provide a method of communicating this information to others. The goal is not to produce an artistic piece of work, nor is it necessary to achieve mapping quickly. A good process map often takes a long time to develop because it includes the interaction of a group of experts, each of whom knows one or two aspects of the process in detail, and needs to learn from others.

Analyzing a Process Map

Once the process map has been drawn, it is often useful to analyze the steps within it. This analysis will vary according to the purpose of the project, but it will often include the classification of each step using value-added codes. Another analysis is to calculate where the costs are accrued, where quality problems are arising, and where delays occur. Useful factors are the value-added percentage (i.e., how much of the total time or cost is expended on value-added tasks) and the ratio of actual cycle time to theoretical cycle time.

It may also be useful to present the map in a way that shows which departments are associated with each step in the process. A simplified example of this is shown in Figure 6.6.

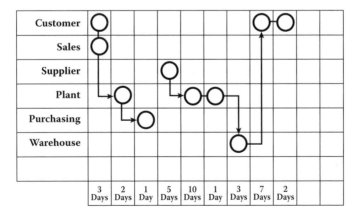

FIGURE 6.6
Process map showing departments.

ROOT-CAUSE ANALYSIS

It is important when creating improvement and reengineering within an organization to get to the root causes of problems. Many improvement projects have floundered because the people on the team have addressed the symptoms and not the root causes of the problems. Once a process map has been drawn and the analysis completed, it is important to analyze the problems and establish the root causes of the issues you are facing.

There are many techniques for establishing root cause, and they must be used appropriately; but the real issue is to spend the time as a team discussing and analyzing the issues, brainstorming the problems, and drilling down into the depth of the situation. Very often, an improvement team will not take the time to do this. People complain about spending too much time in meetings. But the reality is that, in most companies, the issues and problems are deep seated and fundamental, and they do not lend themselves to shallow analysis. Shallow analysis leads to shallow changes, which lead to lack of benefit and lost opportunity.

One technique for root-cause analysis is the use of an *affinity diagram*, on which the people in the team brainstorm the issues associated with a problem, using open-ended starting questions. The purpose is to bring out all the aspects of the problem in a free-form and open manner. Once the ideas are exhausted, then individuals within the team sort these ideas into groups. The grouping is done by several people in turn, until the issues are brought into some clarity. The power of an affinity diagram is that it gives the team the ability to get through to the essence of the problem and provides a foundation for breakthrough solutions.

Another important technique for getting to root causes is the use of *matrix diagrams* to relate different aspects of the issues together (see Table 6.2). The horizontal axis is used to divide the problem into logical pieces (e.g., product families, kinds of customers, markets, kinds of quality problems) and the vertical axis lists the various issues that have been raised. The body of the matrix is used to mark comments and correlation information, to show the degree of cause and effect in each case, to mark the severity of the problem, and so forth. These diagrams are very helpful in clarifying and subdividing a series of problems so they can be better understood and resolved.

TABLE 6.2
Root-Cause Analysis

	Pricing	Cost to Serve	Returns	Quoting Information
Product families	Cost + pricing leads to wrong pricing for each family. Do not differentiate our products.	We do not recapture the costs required for design-to-order or configure-to-order products.	New products have higher level of returns than our traditional products.	The quoting process is the same for all products.
Kinds of customer	Prices are the same for all customers. We do not take account of the needs of different customers and we do not take account of the priority of different customers to our business strategy.	We treat all customers as prime customers. Some customers are more important to us than others. Time spent on lower priority customers takes time away from high priority.	Different kinds of customers have different patterns with regard to returns.	The quoting process is the same for all customers. We do not address the different needs of different customers. We do not recognize that some customers are more important to us than others.
Markets	Again cost+ pricing leads to the same prices used across all of our markets. There are real differences. Price resistance from customers is always met by trying to reduce prices, rather than increase value.	We have no way to recognize the differences of costs required to serve the different markets. Yet it is clear that serving aerospace customers is more complicated and difficult than serving the industrial market, for example.	There are different needs and different criteria for products in different kinds of markets.	We do not have different quoting policies for different markets, despite the fact that the customer needs and value are different.
Quality problems		Different customers and different markets have different quality issues on the same products because they have different policies and needs.	We treat all quality problems in the same way; we panic, expedite, and fawn over the customer. Many returns are not the result of quality problems.	We do not take into account when quoting that there are different needs with regards to specification and quality.
ROOT CAUSES	Cost+ pricing methods. Lack of product and market segmentation.	All customers and products of treated the same way when there are different needs and value.	All customers, markets, and products are regarded the same way. but all returns are not in fact equal.	Cost+ pricing methods. Lack of segmentation of the markets, customers, and product families.
SUGGESTIONS	Need to differentiate our products, customers, and markets more carefully. Need to price to the value of the product to the customer and markets. Develop a standard method for responding to pricing customer pressures.	Establish a method of understanding the different costs associated with serving different kinds of customers and markets with different kinds of products.	Develop different methods to address returns for different kinds of customers according to how different customers value product quality. Develop better understanding of why products are returned.	Develop classifications for combinations of products and markets. Develop different quoting processes for each combination. Introduce value-based pricing.

The classic method of establishing root causes is the *fishbone chart* or the *Ishikawa diagram*. This method was devised by Kaoru Ishikawa (1982), the Japanese quality expert, to provide a simple, effective visual tool for seeing cause and effect. An example of this chart is shown in Figure 6.7. The problem studied is written at the end of the chart, and the primary causes are shown on the first "bones" of the chart. The causes of these primary causes are shown going into the primary "bones," and the next level causes go into the next level "bones." This way, the diagram builds up into an intricate network of causes.

When the team is developing a chart like this, a large piece of paper is fixed to the wall, and Post-It notes are used to attach the causes as they are brought to light through brainstorming. If the primary causes are not easily understood, then it is helpful to use some standard ones (e.g., labor, machines, materials, and methods) as starting points. They can be changed later as the exercise progresses.

The purpose with a cause-and-effect diagram is not to draw an elegant diagram but to uncover the true issues that cause the problems the team is trying to solve or improve.

PROCESS IMPROVEMENT AND REENGINEERING

The primary purpose of a process improvement team is to change the process so that it is better aligned with company strategies and service to the customers, and to trim costs, reduce cycle time, and eliminate quality problems. These objectives require the team to work carefully to understand the process, establish the problems within it, understand the root causes of those problems, and create new processes that will accomplish these goals:

- Eliminate non-value-added tasks and activities
- Eliminate delays and waste
- Eradicate quality problems
- Focus on company strategic goals and service to the customers

The charts and methods described in the previous section are designed to enable the team to better understand the process (via process maps); determine the problems and issues associated with the process (via

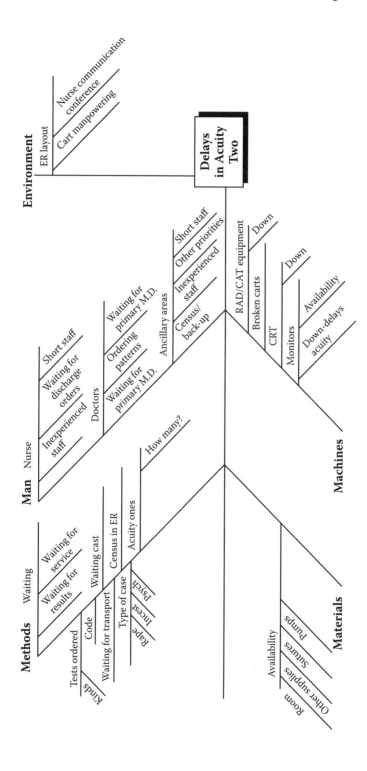

FIGURE 6.7
Fishbone diagram of possible causes of delays.

affinity diagrams); analyze the root causes of the problems (via matrices and fishbone charts); and analyze the cost, cycle time, and quality issues. A systematic method is required to help the team develop new approaches.

These new approaches may be improvements of the current process or they may lead to the development of entirely new, reengineered processes that are a radical departure for the company. Either way, a systematic method of assessing the problems and the potential for improvement is required.

A simple question matrix is helpful here (see Table 6.3) because it forces the team to ask the root questions of what, where, who, when, how, and a number of whys. Some Japanese quality experts advocate the use of "five whys" when analyzing an activity or a process for improvement purposes. The idea is that if you have asked "why" five times over, the team will have gotten to the root of the problem and will not be dealing with surface issues.

Table 6.4 is another set of standard questions that can be used to brainstorm and analyze each step in the process map, with a view to creating an entirely new and better approach.

TABLE 6.3

Example of a Standard Question Matrix

Activity					
What is the purpose?	Why is it necessary?				
Where is it done?	Why is it done here?				
Who does it?	Why is it done by this person or machine?				
When is it done?	Why is it done then?				
How is it done?	Why is it done this way?				

TABLE 6.4

Other Examples of Standard Questions

Can we:	Questions to ask:
Eliminate non-value-added steps?	How is the customer (internal and external) affected by this?
Perform steps in parallel?	How is the supplier (internal and external) affected by this?
Create a U-shaped layout?	Does this step require special training?
Synchronize the steps?	Does this step need documentation?
Simplify the steps?	Is SPC applicable?
Eliminate unneeded motion?	Are all factors known?
Standardize performance?	What are the potential problems in this step?
Mistake-proof the step?	How can we eliminate the cause?
Eliminate transportation or material movement?	If we cannot eliminate the cause, how can it be minimized?
Prevent the problem through planned maintenance?	
Eliminate unsafe operations?	

SUMMARY

The improvement of business processes—both continuous improvement and radical reengineering—requires team-based and systematic methods of analyzing processes and creating improved methods. These analysis methods are valuable for lean improvement, target costing, value engineering, benchmarking, and other improvement methods.

Process mapping is a visual method for charting a business process so that it can be analyzed. Process mapping allows the internal knowledge of the company to be presented and communicated among team members and others. The process map is also a valuable tool for analyzing processes for improvement.

The idea of value-added analysis is to classify activities and tasks within a process to determine which ones create value in the eyes of the customer, and which are wasteful. Non-value-added activities need to be eliminated, and value-added activities need to be improved by making them faster, less costly, and of higher quality.

Real improvement can only come when the improvement team has established the root causes of the problems they are trying to solve. For an improvement project to be successful, it must address and solve the root causes, not the symptoms. The techniques of affinity diagrams, cause-and-effect diagrams, and matrix analysis are useful for drilling down to the root causes.

QUESTIONS

1. What is a process?
2. What are the four different classifications of value-added and non-value-added? Define them.
3. What is the purpose of process mapping?
4. Would team-based storyboarding be useful in your company? What would be the benefits?
5. Which visual tools for root-cause analysis would be most helpful to your organization? Where (i.e., which departments or processes) would you find them most useful?

7

Performance Measurement

Companies need a new approach to performance measurement. As they strive toward world-class performance, the traditional methods of measurement become a hindrance. New measures are needed.

Big changes are taking place in Western industry, and these changes are happening fast. Traditional methods of measuring a company's performance no longer apply. They measure the wrong things, and they mislead people. The issues that are important to world-class companies are:

- Quality
- Productivity
- On-time delivery
- Innovation
- Teamwork
- Flexibility
- Short cycle times
- Closeness to customers

Yet none of these issues is addressed by traditional management accounting measures.

As the needs and expectations of our customers change, so must our measures, to ensure that we are measuring the things our customers value. As management methods change and we move into teamwork approaches, it is important to have measures that follow the same approach. People are led and influenced by the way they are measured. If you measure the right things, people will do the right things. Traditional measures measure the wrong things for companies striving toward a lean transformation. New measures are needed that will lead people in the right direction.

CHARACTERISTICS OF THE NEW PERFORMANCE MEASURES

Many firms have begun to use new performance measures, in line with their world-class approach. Most of these performance measures are not new ideas. But here is what *is* new:

- These measures truly drive the business.
- They replace traditional cost accounting.
- They provide useful input at all levels of the company.

Every firm applies these ideas differently, but common themes can be seen. Measures must conform to the following nine criteria:

1. Relate directly to the business strategy
2. Be primarily nonfinancial
3. Measure the process rather than the outcomes
4. Be presented visually where the work is done
5. Vary based on location
6. Change over time
7. Be simple and easy to use
8. Provide fast feedback of information
9. Foster problem solving and improvement rather than merely monitoring it

The next sections describe each of these requirements in more detail.

What You Measure Should Relate Directly to Business Strategy

World-class companies have clear business strategies. The business strategy of a world-class manufacturer focuses on issues like quality, reliability, short cycle times, flexibility, innovation, customer service, and environmental responsibility. Manufacturing strategy is one element of the company's business strategy, as are new product development and sales and marketing. Each strategy needs performance measures that directly address that strategy.

There are three reasons for keeping performance measures in line with the business strategy.

1. A company needs to know how well it is performing. Therefore, it requires a few measures the managers can use to assess progress.
2. People focus on what you measure. Therefore, if a firm measures and reports someone's work, that person will want to improve his or her work. Similarly, if the performance measures are directly related to the business strategy, the people will be motivated toward the business strategy.
3. Measures provide feedback to help people and teams do their jobs and improve performance.

Figure 7.1 shows typical feedback loops used by lean organizations.

Use Nonfinancial Measures

Traditional firms focus on financial results, whereas lean companies emphasize nonfinancial measures. Accounting reports should not be used for performance measurement. They are not useful for daily control of the business. They are confusing and are often misleading.

For performance measures to be relevant, they must be expressed in terms that directly relate to the business strategy. To disguise the results in

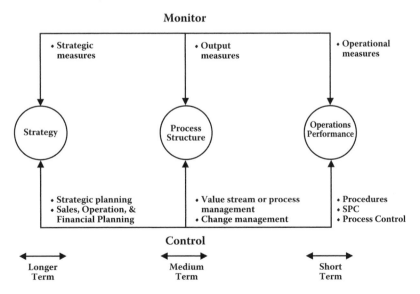

FIGURE 7.1
Links of strategies, processes, and operational performance.

money terms is not helpful. Issues must be measured in terms that make direct sense to the people using them. If the measures are in dollars, the operations people must "translate" dollars into something real. If you want to improve quality, measure quality—not the *cost* of quality. If you are concerned about cycle time, measure cycle time—not labor hour variances.

Measure the Process Rather Than the Outcome

Underlying all lean continuous improvement is the perfection of processes. If you want improved performance, you must improve the process; if you want to improve the process, you must measure the things that demonstrate the capability of the process—not the outcomes, and particularly not the financial outcomes. If you measure and focus on the capability of the process and work to improve the process, then the desired outcomes will be achieved.

Most traditional companies measure and focus on the outcomes and harangue their employees to achieve the "goals." The most common example of this is companies that enforce the achievement of budgeted month-end and quarter-end profits for each division, plant, and location. This always leads to non-lean actions on the part of the managers within the locations, and commonly delays or curtails lean improvement.

Make Sure Measures Are Visually Presented Where the Work Is Done

Visual management is an important part of lean management methods. Some consider visual management to be a primary aspect of "lean culture." People work better when they can see and understand what is going on. Lean performance measurements—particularly at the local cell and value-stream level—are usually gathered and reported and are presented on boards where the work is performed. These measurements are not available anywhere else. Anyone needing to know the cell or value-stream performance can look at the boards.

Managers in lean companies do not run the day-to-day business by sitting in their offices playing with their computers, and they do not have long tedious meetings in anonymous conference rooms. The work of management is done where the real work is done: on the shop floor, in the design office, in the sales office, and so on. Managers in lean companies spend much of their time walking in the areas of their responsibility, watching the processes, studying the measurements, helping to solve problems, and mentoring their people.

Vary Measures to Suit Locations

The way that firms apply lean manufacturing methods varies a lot. Each plant may be different. The products, customers, and employees may differ. Plants in different countries will certainly differ. Obviously, therefore, a standard measurement method does not make sense.

Traditional companies use the same measures everywhere. They often pride themselves on being consistent, and they often compare one plant against another. This is bad: teamwork is vital, and you destroy the team when you judge one against the other. The trend of improvement is the real issue as people work in teams to improve the process. Teams will not work well together if they are rivals. Sharing information and ideas is positive; judging one against another is not.

To bring about major change, you need a "champion," someone who leads the team to success. Two plants that are successful may have different champions with different ideas. The champions will do the job differently. Do not inhibit the champions by making them use standard measures that will not apply to both plants. You will measure the wrong things and also frustrate the champions.

Change Measures over Time

The measures need to change over time. Change is a key to a lean company. All lean firms value continuous improvement, a planned way for all employees to make their work increasingly better. Most changes are small, but when you put them together, they produce a large step forward. When introducing world-class methods, most companies start with a big improvement followed by a continuous improvement program.

Continuous improvement is not a catch phrase; it is a way of life within lean organizations. Continuous improvement means that things change all the time. Therefore, the performance measures must also change. When you start with world-class methods, some issues are more important than others. As time goes by, the important issues will change, so the measures must change to reflect this. See Figure 7.2.

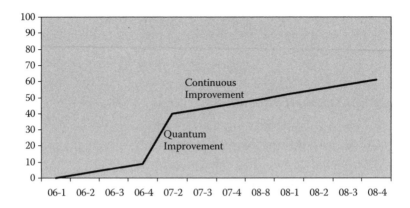

FIGURE 7.2
Improvement measures.

Make Measures Simple and Easy to Use

For performance measures to work, people must understand them. Complex measures do not work. Do not use ratios. Do not use measures combining many aspects into a single factor. These confuse people.

Simple measures of the most important parts of the business are essential. Each issue must be measured directly and presented well. People then find the results easy to use, and the measure is effective.

Performance measures within world-class companies are clear and direct. Often, these measures are made by people on the spot. They use wall charts, bulletin boards, graphs, signals, and computer screens. The best measures are the ones people devise. They understand them and trust the numbers. Even when measures are computer generated, analyzed, and consolidated, they must still be straightforward and easy to use.

Ensure Fast Feedback of Information

Most companies receive their data monthly. These are accounting reports that follow the accounting calendar, but they often arrive too late to be useful. There are often time-wasting meetings to "explain the variances." These meetings force people to defend their actions, not improve performance.

A lean company fixes problems when they happen. It does not wait for a month-end report. The performance measures must help improve performance. To do this, the information is needed fast, sometimes on the spot.

Action cannot wait until the middle of next month. Quality, for example, cannot wait. Other information is needed hourly, twice daily, daily, or weekly. The feedback must match the need.

Foster Improvement Rather Than Merely Monitoring

This last characteristic of performance measurement for a lean company has to do with motivation. Although this measure is intangible, it is of great importance. The performance measurement system will only work if the people using it find it helpful. It will not work if they feel they are being watched and judged.

Performance measures need to show clearly where improvement has been made and where more improvement is possible. Traditional measures are used to judge people. In contrast, lean companies use measures to help people improve. This may sound like a subtle difference, but in practice, it represents the difference between success and failure.

Many of the issues already discussed have an impact on how the measures are used. On-time reports, easy-to-use charts and graphs, direct measurement, and measures that fit the firm's business strategy will help people focus on improvement.

Often, measures are used to blame people or to assess their pay and promotion prospects. This creates fear. A world-class company wants people to be creative, to try out new ideas, to take risks, and ultimately to improve. Fear stops people from improving. The measures must foster improvement.

EXAMPLES OF NEW PERFORMANCE MEASURES AT WORK

There are many approaches to performance measurement. The following examples show how some world-class companies measure performance. However, every company must develop its own measures. There is no standard set.

Do not use too many measures. Most companies measure too much. They work on the assumption that measuring creates more control. This is wrong: the use of too many measures creates confusion and lack of focus.

Therefore, pick six or eight measures that are sufficient to control your business and provide the balance of service, time, quality, and cost.

Measuring Delivery Performance and Customer Service

Every firm has customers. The customers may be the people using the products or services the company makes, or they may be other people within the organization. Although the focus of customer service measures will be the ultimate customer who pays the invoices, even support departments (such as a technical library, for example) have customers within the organization. Measuring the customer's satisfaction is most important.

The best measure of satisfaction is *direct feedback from the customers.* Direct feedback can either be through surveys of the customers or by establishing automatic feedback, such as reply cards, questionnaires, or electronic data interchange (EDI). Reply cards and questionnaires are of limited value because only a few are returned. On the other hand, EDI receipt confirmation is more reliable and does not require additional data entry.

Often, direct feedback is difficult to obtain, and indirect measures—such as on-time shipments—are used to track customer service levels. These measures show the number of on-time deliveries and are usually presented as a graph. An average company will compare the date *promised* with the date shipped. In contrast, a world-class company will show the date the customer *requested* against the date shipped. The customer *need* is what is important—not what was promised.

Do not have too many measures of customer service. Instead, select one measure that addresses the customer's concerns and derive the company's customer service objectives from this single measure. Do not use measures that combine several factors because these confuse people and do not lead to improvement.

Measuring Process Time

A company's operation is, in fact, a series of processes performed repeatedly, and these processes may span more than one department. Manufacturing processes are easily seen, but service and support processes can be more difficult to define. Entering customer orders and meeting the customer needs is a process, as is providing accounting information and designing and enhancing products. All these process times can be measured.

Short process times are essential for world-class companies. Short production process time results in low inventories. Short process times make a company more flexible to the customer's needs. Quick setups and changeovers are essential to short production process times.

World-class companies emphasize timely service to customers, both internal and external. A simple measure is customer service time: the time from receipt of the order to dispatch of the product or service. This is a good measure of how quickly the customers are served. It can often be measured directly from the company's computer systems for order entry and shipping. Or you can count the number of orders in the system that have not yet been shipped, and divide that quantity by the average number of orders shipped per day to calculate the average days of flow.

Manufacturing process times can be measured, sampled, or derived. Most world-class companies do not track a lot of detailed information about processes because it is wasteful. Do not introduce detailed tracking for performance-measurement purposes only; it is non-value-added. Theoretical process times can be derived from production routings or process flow charts, if these documents are accurate and up to date.

Process times can be measured by sampling. For example, every hour, on the hour, everyone stops and measures process time. Every 100th job is measured in detail. Every 10th kanban card is a different color and has space for entry of measurement information on the back of the card. This sample information is gathered, analyzed, and reported on a graph or chart.

Radical reductions in process time are achieved as companies introduce world-class methods. For example:

- A Department of Defense repair operation reduced its process time from 60 days to 8 days.
- A car seat manufacturer reduced customer lead times from 12 weeks to 90 minutes.
- The printed circuit board cell of an electronic equipment manufacturer reduced production cycle times from 1½ weeks to 1 day by introducing cellular manufacturing.

These changes must be tracked and monitored.

Similarly, service and support processes can be measured, for example:

- The time to create invoices (shipment time to invoice transmittal)
- The time to retrieve and deliver a reference book from the technical library
- The time to complete a month-end financial close
- The time to resolve customer service calls

Measuring Innovation

In many industries, innovation is a key to the future. Product life cycles are getting shorter, and the ability to introduce new products, new services, and new procedures is vital. A world-class company emphasizes the need for every individual within the organization to be involved in improvement and innovation. Not only new products must be innovative; new procedures and new services to the customers are also crucial.

How to measure new product innovation varies according to the company and the market. An organization that introduces many new products can continuously measure the rate of new product introduction or the number of new products per month or year. Companies that produce fewer new products can measure the time to market of product. The time to market is defined as the time from conception of the product to its introduction to the marketplace. For example, a Honda Motorcycle plant in Japan introduces one major product enhancement every month. The production process and working hours are geared around this need for new product introduction.

Another slant on innovation is the number of employee suggestions that are made and implemented. Many world-class companies have clearly defined employee suggestion schemes. These methods keep careful track of who suggested what and how it was implemented. Companies that are advanced with these kinds of innovation methods often record the changes after they are made because employees are empowered to make the changes on their own authority. A good measure of suggestions is the number per person per year or month. For example, Toyota Motor Corporation is reported to have achieved around 35 suggestions per person in one year at its production plant in Georgetown, Kentucky.* PSI Corporation, a

---

* Toyota's employee-based approach to improvement has been described in two recent articles: "No Satisfaction at Toyota" (Fishman 2006) and "Toyota: The Open Secret of Success" (Surowiecki 2008)

Connecticut manufacturer of pressure switches for aerospace and defense application, is achieving 40 suggestions per person per year. Even though many of the suggestions are small, they add up to enormous improvement and very high employee involvement and commitment.

Measuring Productivity

The best way to measure productivity in a company or a plant is to measure directly the number of products or services provided per person. When the company has clearly defined value-stream teams, productivity can be measured simply for each value-stream and include all of the people who work in the value-stream. The idea of direct and indirect people is no longer valid; instead, if they work on the value-stream, they are included. It is important to avoid the idea of allocating "equivalent heads" for people who support more than one value-stream, as this only creates confusion, lack of clarity, and triggers meetings to discuss how much and who should be allocated to each value-stream. If they work on the value-stream team, they are included; if they do not, they are excluded. At a plant level, this measurement is simpler. Productivity equals the number of items shipped to customers divided by the number of people working in the value-stream.

Sometimes it is not possible to use this measure because the company's product range includes widely different products, and the mix of products or services provided to customers changes frequently. Often, this can be solved by finding a "common denominator." For example, a company making hydraulic manifolds calculated productivity based on the number of valves because some manifolds had only 2 or 3 valves and others contained 16 or even 32. If all else fails, the measurement can be calculated from the revenue rather than the number of items: i.e., the number of dollars sold per person.

Measuring Flexibility

Flexibility deals with the ability to *make* today what the customers *want* today and changing effectively as customer needs change. Traditional companies meet customer needs by maintaining finished-goods inventories and making to stock. In contrast, lean companies build flexibility into their processes so they can make to order with very short lead times. Measures of flexibility determine a company's ability to meet this demand. Flexibility can be measured, for example, by evaluating any of the following:

- Level of cross training in the plant
- Cycle time from placing an order to shipping the goods
- Degree of commonality of component parts throughout the products
- Degree of common processes across the production floor
- Modularity of the product design
- Position of variability within the products

Measuring Quality

To say that quality is an important aspect of world-class manufacturing is an understatement. Some companies would say that quality *is* world-class manufacturing—that everything else stems from a long-term commitment to improving quality.

Measurement of quality can start with the suppliers. Measuring the quality of incoming material enables you to create reports of vendor quality. However, a world-class company will not want to be doing a lot of incoming inspection of components and raw material because this is a non-value-added activity. The objective is to certify individual suppliers to provide components and raw materials that are up to standard and on time. A measure of the percentage of suppliers certified or the percentage of materials provided by certified suppliers is often helpful.

Production quality is almost always measured in terms of rejects per million items, or first-pass yield. These are straightforward, easy-to-understand methods of measuring quality. Another approach is to measure the number of processes using statistical process control (SPC) and the number of those processes that are "under control."

Customer satisfaction is another good measure of the quality of a product and the quality of the service the customer is receiving. As mentioned earlier in this chapter, customer satisfaction is best measured by direct feedback from surveys. A company with many customers may need to survey a sample number; others can survey all the customers. The key to surveys is to be brief, focused, and address the right people. Some companies use snake charts (see Figure 7.3) because they show customers' opinions of service received and also show the importance they place on each aspect of the service. We may be doing a great job and score very highly on issues the customers consider to be unimportant while scoring poorly on other aspects the customers consider to be of higher significance.

Other quality issues that should be measured involve the accuracy of information within the computer system. You cannot be a world-class manufacturer and maintain high levels of product quality if your information is poor. Primary issues are accuracy in inventory, forecast, bill of materials, and production routing. These issues can be measured as a part of the company's information accuracy maintenance processes like cycle counting and engineering change processing.

Measuring Financial Performance

Although nonfinancial performance measures are better than financial measures, there are some legitimate reasons for using financial measures. The primary reason for using a financial measure is to fill a need for a common denominator to consolidate dissimilar information on a single report. There are two cautions when using financial performance measures.

The first is that the definition of the financial information needs to be determined carefully. Often, standard costs, sales figures, market value, and the like are used to present the information, which can be quite misleading.

Importance	1	2	3	4	5	6	7	8	9	10
Score	1	2	3	4	5	6	7	8	9	10
On-time delivery										
Reliability										
Lead time										
Emergency orders										
"Hot-line" support										
Brand name										

FIGURE 7.3
Customer-service snake chart.

The second caution is that many companies use financial reports to make comparisons of plants, locations, and departments. These comparisons are not compatible with a world-class approach, where teamwork and continuous improvement are emphasized. Teamwork breaks down when judgmental comparisons are made among plants or departments. Similarly, the issue is not the actual value of the measure, but the way it changes over time. If you are using financial measures so that comparisons can be made, stop it and develop nonfinancial measures that are appropriate to the different needs of the locations.

Performance measures can be shown in financial terms when a common denominator is required to summarize heterogeneous data such as the scrap value of a wide variety of components or products (see Figure 7.4). Useful financial measures include scrap reporting, inventory turns derived from financial information, value-added ratios, and product costs and profitabilities.

Measuring Social Issues

We all recognize that the issues of teamwork, morale, leadership, and participation are of crucial importance to a world-class company, yet these issues are difficult to measure. Traditional measures make no attempt to address these issues and focus on the "bottom line." There are, however, a number of approaches that companies use to gauge their success in these areas.

Morale and teamwork can be measured using the time-honored negative parameters of employee turnover, productive days lost through absenteeism, etc. More positive measures of morale and teamwork can be derived from direct measures of involvement in participation activities. Here are some other good measures to consider:

- Percentage of people on participation teams (if these teams are voluntary)
- Number of suggestions per person
- Number of suggestions implemented
- Amount of education or number of training classes taken per person
- Average number of certified skills per person within the plant or office

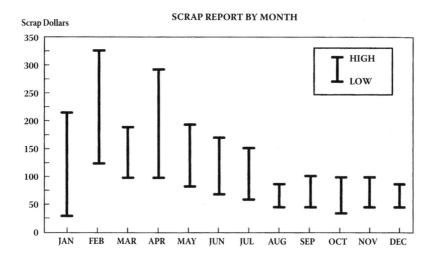

FIGURE 7.4
Scrap reporting using "upper and lower" charts.

Leadership can be measured using personnel surveys and work environment measures. These measures vary from highly complex sociological surveys to straightforward questionnaires. One of the complex measures is the Stanford Work Environment Scale, which uses three questionnaires to measure such issues as involvement, peer cohesion, and autonomy. Simpler forms have been devised by such organizations as Kodak and the U.S. Census Bureau. These forms ask straightforward questions, such as "Does your manager provide you with adequate training?" and "Do you feel part of a team in your department?"

World-class companies are very concerned about safety and environmental issues. They often establish safety and environmental audits within the organization. These audits are typically more stringent than government regulations and are conducted on a regular basis throughout the organization. Reports show the degree to which each department or area is adhering to the company's safety and environmental code.

IMPLEMENTING NEW PERFORMANCE MEASUREMENTS

A new measurement system is a major change and must be introduced with great care. Do not be tempted to do a "quick and dirty" implementation.

Changing measures changes the way people work. What you measure is what you get.

There are eight steps required to establish a new approach to performance measurement:[*]

1. Establish a clear understanding of the strategic issues.
2. Set goals and objectives for each strategic area.
3. List the critical success factors (CSFs) required to achieve the strategic issues.
4. Validate the critical success factors.
5. Link the critical success factors to the company's value-streams and other key processes.
6. Develop key measures for each critical success factor.
7. Use the measures in a "pilot" area.
8. Expand the measures to the whole plant or company.

The remainder of this chapter describes each step in more detail.

Step 1: Write a Strategy

The starting point for the development of new performance measures is a clear understanding of the company's strategies. A common mistake when developing new performance measures is to jump too quickly to the development of measures. Understanding the company's strategies is a foundation for developing strategically based performance measures (see Figure 7.5).

Step 2: Set Goals and Objectives for Each Strategic Issue

Defining strategic issues is helpful for clarifying where the company needs to go, but it is necessary to also develop goals and objectives for these strategies to become reality. The next step is to establish, through the company's senior managers, the goals and objectives for each strategic issue. A strategy is only a good idea if it has no clearly defined goals and no plan to achieve them. Objectives state the *qualitative direction* in which the company wishes to go, and the goals state the *quantitative outworking* of those objectives.

---

[*] A more detailed explanation and examples are given in Chapter 19 of *Practical Lean Accounting* (Maskell and Baggaley 2004).

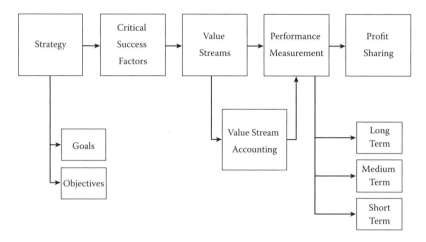

FIGURE 7.5
Development of strategy-based performance measurements.

Spend the time to get these goals and objectives right. Often, the team will be treading on politically dangerous ground. It is better to stir up the political ambiguities of the organization at this stage than to continue to pretend. A world-class or agile company will be determined to match reality to rhetoric.

Step 3: List the Critical Success Factors

Once a strategy is written, the critical success factors (CSFs) can be defined. The CSFs are the actions by the company that make the strategy real. The strategy is the path to success. The CSFs are the stepping stones on the path.

Make a list of what must be done to put the strategy into action. Review it carefully with the people responsible for making things happen. Managers, shop-floor people, office workers, and people in the field all need to be included. There needs to be clarity of understanding within the company so that everyone moves in the same direction and understands why. The new performance measures must augment the company's strategic direction, and they can do so only if the CSFs are clearly understood.

Step 4: Validate the Critical Success Factors

Stating critical success factors does not mean that the company is serious about implementing them. Having established the critical success factors linked to each strategy, it is important to validate to what extent these CSFs are applied within the company. Make a list of the actions the company has taken to make each strategic improvement a reality.

Many companies pay lip service to such issues as serving the customer, providing high quality, and achieving world-class service; however, only tangible actions make a strategy real. Check that you are really taking steps to bring the strategy to life before building a performance measurement program.

Step 5: Link the CSFs to Value-Streams and Other Key Processes

All company activities are processes, and it is important to understand which processes affect the CSFs of the business, because these are the processes that need to be understood and improved (see Figure 7.6). Once the CSFs have been understood and agreed on by the people involved, then the team needs to establish a list of the processes that make up the CSFs.

The company's primary processes will be the:

- Order-fulfillment value-streams
- New product development value-streams
- Sales and marketing value-streams

There may also be some other key support processes that are not contained within the value-streams.

Step 6: Develop Key Measures

Once the strategy is well understood and validated, the CSFs are established, and the value-streams supporting the CSFs are understood, you are ready to start developing new measures.

In general, a company requires three levels of performance measures:

1. *Operational measures* control the day-to-day work on the shop floor or warehouse, in the offices, and out in the field. They are taken frequently by the people doing the job and are posted visually at the

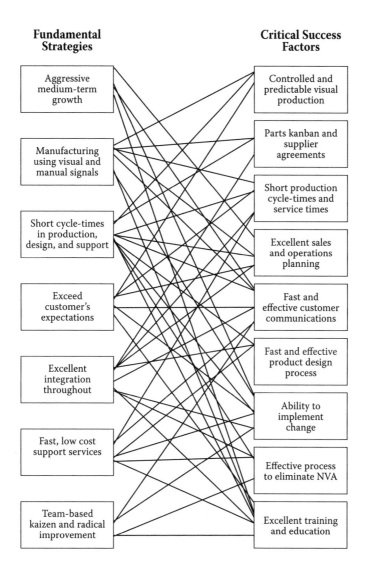

FIGURE 7.6
Strategies linked to CSFs.

cell, department, or office. These measurements accomplish all of the following:

- They control the processes
- They identify problems or process defects
- They initiate the solution of these problems

2. *Value-stream (or process) measures* control the value-streams that provide success for the company's objectives. Value-stream measurements are primarily used to monitor the success of the streams and to drive the improvement of the streams. Value-stream measurements are typically reported weekly by the team members and are posted.

3. *Strategic (plant or division) measures* track and control the company's success at putting the strategies into action, and they are taken less frequently for use by the senior managers.

Every measure must meet the nine criteria discussed earlier in this chapter and define the following for each measurement:

- Link each measure to a CSF.
- Think about the format for reporting the measure.
- Where will the data come from?
- How easily can you gather the data?
- What makes this a good measure?
- What are the weaknesses of the measure?
- Can the measure be consolidated across departments or cells?

The best measures are reported directly by the people using them, and they use data that is already available for other reasons. Some companies make that a rule. It is wasteful to gather data for performance measurement alone.

The best measures are presented visually. Pictures are better than words or numbers. Plan the format carefully. Can the people using the measures draw their own charts? Are the measures flexible enough to meet the needs of each cell or department? Do you need different measures for each cell or department?

Some companies focus on presentation. They do not specify how the measures should be calculated, only how they should be presented. For example, every department must report its quality, throughput time, cost, and customer service. The results must be shown on four graphs presented on a single sheet of paper. Each cell or department devises its own measures, but they all present them in the same format. By the same token, if consolidation is important, it is best to gather and report the measured data through a computer system.

Step 7: Pilot the New Performance Measures

As with most significant changes, it is best to try a new measure before committing to it. Start using the new performance measures in a pilot area of the company. Select a self-contained part of the business, develop the measures, and put them into practice. The pilot will reveal any shortcoming, as well as showing how a new approach to measurement is helpful.

Step 8: Expand the Measures to the Whole Plant or Company

Once the pilot has shown that the new measures work well, expand them to the entire plant. This will require abandoning the old measures. This is where the "rubber meets the road." It takes courage to abandon the old measures, but it must be done. *You cannot have two performance measurement systems running at the same time.*

Make sure the people using the new measures have been trained. It is important to show people why the new measures are better. If the new measures present a bigger challenge, you will have to provide more training and more education. Have the team people available for informal training and encouragement.

SUMMARY

New performance measures are required when a company moves from traditional approaches into world-class methods. The old approach was heavily biased toward financial measures and did not focus on the real issues that create value and service to the customers and wealth to the company. Frequently, the traditional measures focused on issues that made people do things that were positively harmful to the business.

A new approach to performance measures requires understanding the company's business strategies and the critical success factors (CSFs) that can make the strategy a reality. From this understanding, a team-based performance-measurement development project can be initiated. The new measures will be strategically based, primarily nonfinancial, and can change over time and from one part of the company to another. They will be easy to use, provide fast and effective feedback, and will foster improvement rather than merely monitor the business.

The development of these kinds of performance measures starts with studying the company's strategies and understanding the CSFs of the organization. These CSFs are linked to the company's primary business processes, and then goals and objectives are established. This analysis is difficult to do and requires the liaison and cooperation of many people throughout the company. It is essential that this process be real and not simply "window dressing."

The easiest part of the process is the development of the performance measures themselves. Once the analysis has been done thoroughly, the performance measures appear readily. The new measures must adhere to the eight criteria listed at the beginning of this chapter and discussed in detail throughout.

QUESTIONS

1. Are the performance measures used by your company directly linked to your company's strategies?
2. What are your company's primary strategies? List them, and think through which critical success factors affect these strategies most profoundly.
3. Do your current measures adhere to the eight criteria for performance measurement presented in this chapter?
4. Can you control your company's value-streams with six or fewer measures? What would they be?

8

A New Approach to Product Design

In recent years, forward-thinking companies have been approaching product design in a very different way. These approaches vary from company to company, but they can be grouped under the heading of *concurrent engineering*. The objectives of concurrent engineering include:

- Reduced design time
- Improved product quality
- Improved profitability by reducing design costs, manufacturing costs, and product life-cycle costs
- Design for ease of manufacture
- Meeting or exceeding customer requirements and expectations

We must get better at designing products if we are to be competitive. There are some clear trends emerging, including product proliferation, short time to market, and mass customization. Let's look at each of these trends, before moving on to a detailed discussion of a new approach to product design.

With respect to *product proliferation*, there are many more products being introduced now than in previous years. The explosion of new products over the last 10 years has been caused by rapid technology changes, the customer's demand for more individuality, and marketing needs for differentiation and novelty. This has placed demands on product design and development, production, the supply chain, and the financial analysis of product and customer profitability. These changes require the ability to rapidly design and introduce new products into the market at the right time, the right price, the right cost, and in accordance with customer needs.

What are often overlooked are the increasing costs associated with the maintenance of a much wider range of products. Few companies have systematic methods for removing unnecessary products as new products are introduced. Variety is always seen as a benefit, whereas the increased complexity of wide and rapidly changing product families often leads to additional costs and lower customer value.

Shorter time to market is also a major trend: for example, it used to take Chrysler Corporation about eight years to design a new car from concept to showroom. This was standard for the industry. The innovative Chrysler Concorde range of cars was designed from scratch and took less than 39 months. This matches the design cycles of Nissan, Toyota, and other world-class companies.

In some industries, for example consumer electronics, it is vital to be first to market with a new product idea. Profitability depends to a large extent on being first in the marketplace. Quality is important, good design is important, good marketing and customer support processes are important. But profitability over the product's life cycle is significantly affected by time of entry into the market.

Finally, with respect to the trend toward *mass customization*, consumer goods manufacturers used to have a focused range of products that were sold through retailers to the public. However, these days, the major retailers want their own custom products, and not only self-labeled products, but products with different features and functions that meet the needs of their target customers.

Similarly, suppliers in every kind of industry are finding that their customers increasingly require small quantities of customized products instead of buying "standard" items. This trend toward customized products (and the agile manufacturing methods required to produce them) is a major change taking place in Western manufacturing. The term mass customization was coined to describe this trend (Pine 1993).

WHAT IS WRONG WITH THE TRADITIONAL DESIGN APPROACH?

The traditional approach to design takes too long and is too expensive. It requires considerable redesign at each stage, relies on pilot production to "iron out" the problems, and is often not customer focused.

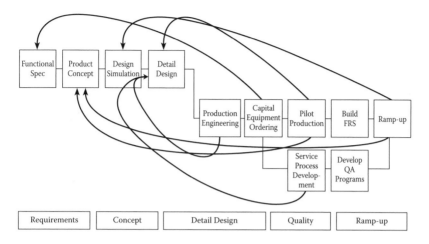

FIGURE 8.1
Traditional "over the fence" design.

Figure 8.1 shows a typical traditional design process, sometimes called "over-the-fence" design because each department works separately and then throws the design over the fence to the next department. Traditional design processes take a long time because the work is done sequentially, i.e., one department followed by the next, followed by the next.

Here are a few of the problems with the traditional approach:

- *It is too long* because it takes a long time to process the design through each department and to complete the reviews and redesigns required.
- *It is too expensive* because there are many redesign activities as other departments identify shortcomings of the original design. This results in many changes taking place later in the process. Changes are more complex and expensive when they are made later in the design process.
- *It is likely to produce a poorer quality product* because it fails to take into account, during the *early* stages of design, the following factors:
  Needs of customers
  Manufacturing process
  Customer service department
  Quality assurance people

These needs are patched in later in the process, which inevitably leads to a less satisfactory result.

CONCURRENT ENGINEERING
- Shortening lead times
- Raising quality

CONCURRENT ENGINEERING

How Concurrent Engineering Improves on Traditional Design

Concurrent engineering (also called *simultaneous* or *parallel engineering*) seeks to eliminate the problems of traditional design by having all the departments work together as a team to design a new product. This approach is faster because the development tasks are done in parallel, and much of the waiting and paper shuffling is eliminated.

Concurrent engineering also results in better designs because the early design work takes account of the needs of production, quality, marketing, customer service, and other areas critical to the product's success. Therefore, it is possible to design the product for ease of manufacture, to design high quality into the product, and to make the product easier to support after the sale. If these issues are addressed in the functional and conceptual stages of the design, the result is a better product.

Concurrent engineering also reduces the cost of developing a new product. Figure 8.2 shows a typical pattern of development costs. Despite incurring the largest costs later in the design process, the majority of costs are committed in the early stages. Concurrent engineering seeks to minimize these costs by having a wide range of people contribute to these decisions in the early stages.

The elimination of pilot production is an important objective of concurrent engineering. If a company is introducing new products much more quickly, it cannot afford the time and disruption to produce pilots. To eliminate pilots, the design must be done "right the first time." The quality, production, marketing, and customer service issues must be

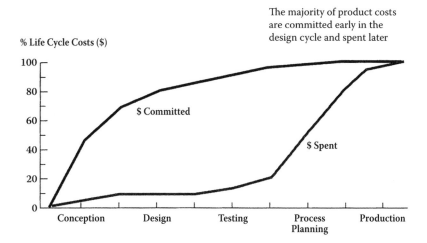

FIGURE 8.2
Life-cycle time and costs.

dealt with up front so that the design is right before the product goes into production.

Figure 8.3 shows the spread of engineering changes with a concurrent engineering approach. Instead of many ECNs (engineering change notices) applied after production has started (which is the most complex and expensive time to implement engineering changes), the emphasis is on getting all the design changes done early in the process.

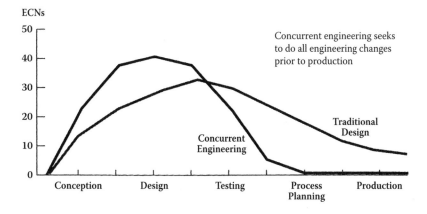

FIGURE 8.3
Engineering changes during design.

Methods of Concurrent Engineering

Concurrent engineering is not easy. It requires excellent project planning and management skills. It requires good cooperation between the various departments of the company. It requires teamwork, attention to detail, vision, commitment, and very high standards (Hartley 1992). These are all attributes that differentiate world-class companies from traditional companies.

Some of the keys to success are described in the following subsections.

Cross-Functional Teams

Concurrent engineering requires teams of people from different disciplines working together. Each person brings his or her own specialty, but each is also part of the team and is involved with activities outside of his or her own specific responsibilities. Often customers and suppliers are included in these teams. The management accountant also has a vital role to play in a concurrent design team.

Integrated Approach

This is the opposite of the "over the fence" design method. The project is organized so that each aspect of the design can be achieved concurrently. Everyone is involved with bringing the product to market quickly and perfectly. This requires excellent integration of the work. There is no less work to do; it must be integrated into a tight schedule.

Detailed Analysis

There is no substitute for doing all the homework. One reason traditional companies use pilots to highlight problems is that their design process does not look at the issues in enough detail. In contrast, part of the concept of total quality management is paying very close attention to what causes problems and solving these root causes. This must be the approach to concurrent engineering if the design is to be "right the first time."

Customer-Focused Design

A major benefit of concurrent engineering is that the cross-functional team has the people required to handle all the important aspects of the design.

Successful concurrent engineering teams focus on the needs of the customer. The customer has quality needs, feature and function needs, and price needs. The price is almost always driven by the needs of the customer.

Tough-to-Reach Targets

Concurrent engineering teams usually set themselves tough goals that include cost targets, quality targets, time-to-market targets, and product functional targets that are set early in the process and then refined as the design takes shape. The accountants are involved in target-setting tasks.

The benefits of a concurrent engineering approach reach to every part of the company:

- Increased customer satisfaction
- Increased market share
- Faster time-to-market
- Few engineering changes
- Reduced total lifetime costs
- Reduced design costs
- Reduced manufacturing costs
- Reduced warranty costs
- Improved communications within the company
- Improved cooperation with suppliers

Role of the Accountant in Product Design

There are exciting new roles for accountants as their companies move into new product design methods like concurrent engineering. There are new techniques to be learned and used, including:

- Target costing
- Value engineering
- Life-cycle costing
- Quality function deployment
- Variety-effectiveness analysis
- Continuous improvement

In addition to applying these techniques, the accountant also makes a contribution as a team member. The analytical skills of accountants lend themselves well to product design teams. This is the strength of a cross-functional team: people from different disciplines bring their own perspectives to the task. This creative synergy of a diverse group is powerful, and it is one of the reasons why concurrent engineering teams create better designs.

TARGET COSTING

- Used in product planning and design
  - Involves cost planning, not cost control
  - Matches product costs to customer needs and company needs prior to production
- Used for product costs, research and development costs, and postproduction usage costs

---

TARGET COSTING

Target costing starts with an understanding of the market. The target costs for a new product are derived from the price the customers are willing to pay for the product. Accountants work with sales and marketing to understand the parameters of the market and make a judgment about the price the market will bear. If the new product is a variation of a current product, then the market price may be assessed quite easily. If the product is entirely new, it is more difficult to determine the market price.

The company will have established a policy of how much gross profit it wishes to make on a product. By subtracting the target profit from the sales price, the allowable cost can be calculated. The allowable cost is the product cost required to achieve the target profit the company wishes to make.

Based on the current design of the new product, which may be very early in the design process, the current estimated cost can be determined. Early in the process, these estimated costs may be unreliable. As the design progresses, the estimated costs will become firmer figures. The difference between the allowable cost and the estimated cost is called the *cost gap*. During the design process, this cost gap must be bridged if the company is to achieve its desired profit. The role of the accountant on the team is to work with the engineers and other team members to achieve the allowable cost.

In practice, the allowable cost is often far less than the current estimated cost. To establish the allowable cost as a goal in the early stages of the design would be to set an unattainable objective that would not serve a useful purpose. The accountants establish target costs for the product or for major subassemblies of the product. The target costs must be within reach of the team, but they must also be aggressive goals.

Early in the design process, the target costs will be established for the product and for major pieces of the product. For example, there will be a target cost for an automobile model made up of the targets for the body, the transmission, the motor, and other major subassemblies. Later in the design process, the target costs will be applied to a lower level and include components and smaller subassemblies. It is often not necessary to establish targets for every part. The level of target costing is a judgment that must be made by the team.

The targets themselves also change over time. The purpose of the targets is to provide the design team with a tough but attainable cost goal. The team uses design techniques and value-engineering analysis to bring the estimated cost in line with the target. As soon as you attain the target, the target is moved. Once the team has built the target costs into the product design, the accountants (in liaison with the rest of the team) establish a more aggressive set of targets. This procedure is repeated throughout the design processes until the estimated cost is brought into line with the allowable cost. The company's profit goals can then be satisfied.

Target costing (Monden 1992; Sakurai 1992; Cooper and Slagmulder 1997) is a systematic method for establishing motivating goals for the team that are tough yet attainable, and that are based on real data developed within the team. These targets are not set by outsiders. They are set by the team members themselves, who are then committed to their successful achievement. The accountants on the team not only establish the target costs, but they are responsible, as team members, to make them a reality.

Target costing is not used solely for product costing. Targets are also set for the cost of the design process itself, postproduction issues like distribution costs, and sometimes for the usage and disposal costs that are incurred by the customer. This way, the team is able to keep focused on the needs of the customer and the larger needs of the organization. A recent survey of Japanese companies that used target costing showed that less than half of the target costs were related to the product costs themselves; the other target costs were related to the design, distribution, and use of the products.

VALUE ENGINEERING

The systematic, team-based method used to bring actual costs into line with target costs.

VALUE ENGINEERING

Value engineering is a set of formal techniques used to bring the design into line with the target costs. These techniques provide a planned and orderly approach to the assessment of product costs throughout the design process. The formal definition of value engineering is as follows:

> Value engineering is an activity *to design a product from many different angles, to meet the customer's needs, and to meet the organization's objectives*, at the lowest possible cost.

The processes and procedures of value engineering vary considerably from one organization to another, depending on the products designed and the needs of the market. But the essential elements are that the design engineers, production engineers, field service engineers (if necessary), purchasing people, suppliers, and accountants work together in a team to eliminate cost from the design of the product or segments of the product. This is done through careful analysis of what drives the costs, innovative engineering (both design and process), and cooperative material sourcing.

In the early stages of a product design, the target costs will be established at a macro level. The finished product will be broken down into its major assemblies, and a target cost will be established for each major assembly. Value engineering methods will be used to bring the cost of the major assemblies into line with the target before the detailed design is started. As the design progresses and the individual component parts and their production processes are designed, value engineering is used to optimize the costs of each lower-level part and subassembly.

An important skill required of the accountant in this process is the ability to create accurate estimated costs throughout the design process. These costs cannot be "rolled up" in the traditional way because the product has not yet been fully designed. The accountant must use analogy with other similar products, heuristic cost forecast methods, and educated guesses throughout this process. Therefore, it is imperative that the accounting people involved with value engineering have a good understanding of the engineering associated with the product design. They must understand the production processes, the characteristics of the materials used, the software, machine tools, jigs, fixtures, etc. It is not necessary for the accountants to become engineering experts, but they must have a good understanding of the products and processes they are working on.

LIFE-CYCLE COSTING
- Provides a long-term perspective for product design
- Allows better strategic decision making
- Maximizes profits over the product's lifetime

LIFE-CYCLE COSTING

The purpose of life-cycle costing during product design is to provide a broader view of the product costs. As product ranges increase and the life cycle of individual products gets shorter, it becomes more important to understand the costs of designing, developing, manufacturing, and distributing product families rather than individual products. Similarly, as products become increasingly complex and the technology costs increase, it becomes important to understand the total costs of a product over its entire life cycle instead of just knowing the immediate production costs.

Life-cycle costing has been important in some industries for many years. For example, pharmaceutical manufacturers incur enormous research and development costs that frequently produce no direct results at all. The development costs of new pharmaceuticals are very high and can encompass many years of work. These costs must be understood in light of the costs and revenues of the products over their entire lifetimes and in the many marketing forms the product takes.

Marketing people are concerned with lifetime costs. The launch of a new product or product family is often preceded by an analysis of the expected revenues and costs over the number of years the product is expected to be sold. Marketing plans and approaches require a long-term view.

The ultimate goal of life-cycle costing is to enable the designers, engineers, manufacturers, marketers, and company executives to make decisions that will maximize the profit made from a product (or product family) over the lifetime of the product. Life-cycle costing affects many aspects of strategic decision making, including pricing, profit objectives, product development plans, and product retirement plans.

Life-cycle costing also relates the new product or product family to a broader organizational perspective. The marketers, designers, engineers, and manufacturing people involved with the project can see the new product in the context of the company's product range and corporate aspirations.

Figure 8.4 shows the four stages of a product's life cycle: startup, growth, maturity, and decline. The costs associated with each stage are significantly different, and it is important for the accountant to have an understanding of how these costs change over time.

Better decisions can be made when the life-cycle costs and profitabilities are understood. A product's location within its life cycle can impact decisions associated with all of the following factors and issues:

- Product differentiation
- Pricing

	STARTUP	GROWTH	MATURITY	DECLINE
Objective	Sales Growth	Sales Growth	Profits	Cash Flow/Profits
Perf. Measure	Quality Service	Quality Service	Price	Price
Product R & D	High	Moderate	Moderate	Low
Process R & D	Moderate	High	High	Low
Advertising	Moderate	High	Moderate	Low
Plant and Equipment	Low	High	Moderate	Low

FIGURE 8.4
Aspects of the product life cycle.

- Risk assessment
- Market entry
- Market share
- Marketing strategy
- Production volumes
- Product performance
- Product abandonment

Including Usage Costs in Life-Cycle Costing

Some companies examine product life-cycle costs from the company's perspective and from the customer's perspective: the *company* is concerned with profitability over the life cycle of the product, whereas the *customer* is concerned with the product's performance at a given price. The customer is also concerned with the cost of using the product. The product may require maintenance or repair; it may need special installation; it may need fuel or other items added to it; and there may be a cost of finally disposing of the product. To fully understand the product's place in the market and its overall cost and profitability, the company must understand the life-cycle costs from the customer's perspective as well.

For instance, the public is increasingly concerned about environmental and ecological issues. Companies concerned to understand the lifetime profitability of their products are taking life-cycle costing a step further by including *societal costs* into their cost models. This approach is currently in its early stages, but there is every sign that government and other institutions will be requiring a more comprehensive view of the cost and benefits of a product. For example, if every company were required, at its own expense, to dispose of its products after the customer had finished using them, disposal would have a significant impact on the design and promotion of the company's products. Some of the more progressive companies are using life-cycle costing to assess these issues today so they can be a step ahead of this trend.

Calculating Life-Cycle Costs

The big issue with life-cycle costing in the design stages of a product is that it is very difficult to determine the costs and revenues of a product over its life cycle. Like any forecast, life-cycle costs are always wrong. Sometimes, they are very wrong. However, this should not deter us from calculating these costs, because the accuracy will improve over time.

The first step toward developing a lifetime cost model is to do a detailed breakdown of the cost contributors. This is where life-cycle costing integrates with target costing and value-stream costing. Many of the cost contributors required for life-cycle costing forecasts will have already been identified as a part of the target-costing analysis. Similarly, as the target-costing activities become more detailed and precise throughout the design process, so the life-cycle cost forecasts can develop in scope and detail.

It is important when developing a life-cycle cost model to have a thorough understanding of the market. This is where the accountants will work with the sales and marketing personnel to determine where the product fits in the marketplace, what this product brings that differentiates it from other similar products, and what the customers' patterns of purchase will be. Customer usage and product disposal costs will also be assessed at this time. Forecasts of future revenues will be established based upon this market analysis.

The assessment of product costs and how they will change over time is not a precise science. There are three approaches that can be used:

1. Analogy
2. Parametric modeling
3. Industrial engineering

Life-cycle costing is a relatively new technique, and companies are experimenting with new methods of cost assessment. Let's look at each of these in a bit more detail.

The *analogy method* uses historical information from another product that has similar characteristics to the new product (or product family). The assumption is made that the cost patterns observed in the analogous product will be repeated in the new product. This approach is quick and easy to use (provided that the historical information is readily available) and the costs are based on something "real."

The downfall of the method is, of course, finding analogous products. It is often impossible to find a single product that can reliably represent the pattern of the new product. Sometimes, it is necessary to combine the historical data from more than one product to build up the pattern of cost over the product's life cycle; but it is difficult to be confident that the analogous pattern is valid.

The *parametric modeling* method is gaining popularity for life-cycle costing. These models, which were originally developed for economic analysis, seek to understand the parameters that drive costs and revenues, and they use projections of the values of these parameters to determine the life-cycle costs. In a simple example of this approach, a company making baby products will carefully consider birth rate projections and family demographics when developing new products. Another example is the reliance of manufacturers of construction materials on forecasts of building starts.

Parametric modeling can provide excellent results if the parameters are well understood. Another advantage is that the projections used are often available to the public from government and academic research organizations and do not require costly research by the company.

These models, however, are often very complex and subtle. Specialized skills are required to develop and maintain such models. The complexity increases dramatically as the number of parameters increases because the interrelationship between the parameters must be understood. Powerful computers and sophisticated programs are required to develop the model and to perform the sensitivity analysis that is needed to validate the model and to assess its accuracy.

The third approach is the traditional *industrial engineering cost "rollup."* Once the product is designed in detail, it is possible for the detailed costs to be calculated from the product's bill of materials and production process. Other costs, such as transportation costs and disposal costs, can be calculated from the physical characteristics of the product. Future changes in such issues as labor costs, fuel costs, material costs, etc., can be made so that the total product costs can be projected over the life cycle of the product.

This method cannot be used until the product is fully designed. It requires a considerable amount of time and effort to roll up all the costs associated with the product and create the final life-cycle model. However, this approach is well understood and has obvious validity to the people using the numbers.

Whichever method (or combination of methods) is used, it is important to realize that these projections are far from accurate. They do, however, provide a better basis for decision making than no information at all. Companies using life-cycle costing for strategic purposes find that it is important to constantly revise their projections as real data becomes available. In the early stages of product launch, the incoming data will not be very helpful, but once reliable information is established, the life-cycle cost model can be continuously updated and refined.

Owing to the nature of a life-cycle cost model, it is vital that the model be developed by a cross-functional team and not by the accountants alone. This is an example of the power of a concurrent engineering team composed of people from many different disciplines within the company.

QUALITY FUNCTION DEPLOYMENT (QFD)

A formal approach to hearing the voice of the customer throughout the design and product development process.

QUALITY FUNCTION DEPLOYMENT

Quality function deployment (QFD) is a formalized method of matching the expressed needs of the customer to the features and functions of the product. Classic QFD uses a diagram called the "house of quality" (see Figure 8.5), which lists the customer's expectations of the product down the left-hand side of the chart. The planned product features are shown on the chart and matched to customer needs. The chart also shows other aspects, such as competitive analysis, functional interaction, and priorities. This sophisticated visual method keeps the team's eyes squarely focused on the customer needs.

The following list describe the steps required for a QFD project:

Step 1: Assess customer needs. This can be done through a market research survey, by interviews with current customers, or by less direct methods. It is vital to have good customer needs information. When drawing the chart, it is helpful to use the customer's exact words as much as possible.

Step 2: Categorize customer needs. For purposes of clarity, the customer's expressed needs are organized into different categories by the

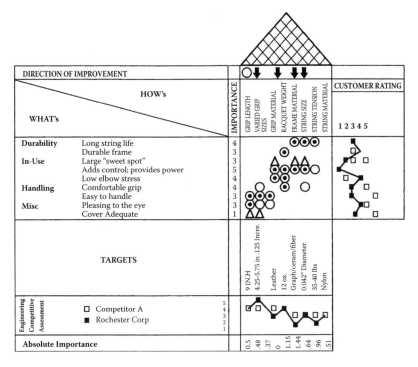

FIGURE 8.5
Example of a QFD house chart. (From Stocker 1992. Reprinted by permission.)

team. The use of an affinity diagram is often helpful for this task (Mizuni 1979).

Step 3: Prioritize customer needs. Each item on the list is prioritized according to importance. It may be necessary to go back to the customer for input at this stage. A simple prioritizing method with scores from 1 to 5 is best.

Step 4: Perform current competitive analysis. This is a "reality check" to see how your current products compare to competitive products based on customer needs.

Step 5: Establish relationships. As the design project progresses, it is important to show how the features of the design relate to the customer's expressed needs. The features of the newly designed product are entered onto the chart, and matches are established to show how these features meet the customer's needs.

Step 6: Assess the importance of design requirements. The importance of each design requirement can be assessed from the importance the customer places on a feature and the degree to which each feature provides a competitive edge.

Step 7: Correlate design requirements. The roof of the house chart is used to show the correlation between design features: which augment each other and which are contrary to each other.

From this systematic analysis, the final chart can be drawn. QFD charts are usually drawn by hand, and they are often drawn and redrawn throughout the development process. The purpose of the exercise is not to create pretty pictures, but to involve the team in a study of how the product matches the customer's needs.

The accountants on the team often prove adept at the use of house charts. Despite the technical nature of the features discussed, the accountants and other professionals can provide analysis and support to the engineers in matching the needs of the customers to the features of the product.

VARIETY EFFECTIVENESS ANALYSIS

As the number of products a company manufactures increases, there is a considerable challenge in coping with all the different parts, processes, and products. Henry Ford was able to be amazingly productive by having a single product (his motto was, "Any color you want, providing it's black") and perfecting the production process for that single product. Today's manufacturers must be as effective as Ford (or better) with a wide variety of products.

There is both a positive and a negative aspect to variety:

- *Positive variety* is the ability to offer customers a wider range of custom or focused products.
- *Negative variety* is the complexity and confusion caused by having many different products, processes, components, and distribution channels.

We need to be able to provide positive variety to our customers while limiting the negative variety effects on the production and distribution processes.

An example of negative variety is taken from a Canadian company that manufactures drilling bits for oil rigs and other deep-drilling facilities.

This company had 15 product families of drilling bits, each containing several different kinds of bits. These families each had different engineering characteristics. A product rationalization program revealed that the customers were bewildered by the variety of bits available and were uncertain when to use each kind.

So this company redesigned its products, which reduced its product line to only three product families. Each of these families was then reengineered to fill a broad range of tasks. The customers were happy because they only had to stock 3 different kinds of drilling bits instead of 15. In turn, the company gained substantial savings by making, stocking, and marketing far fewer products.

Similarly, electronics companies often find significant duplication of parts and components: the same item with more than one part number, and interchangeable components that are shown separately. For example, one company had 1,500 different item numbers for resistors, and 120 of these were 1,000-ohm resistors. Through a detailed variety-effectiveness program, the company reduced its resistor item list from 1,500 to 200.

The savings associated with this reduction were enormous. Many of the savings were intangible and difficult to quantify and included such things as reducing complexity and confusion within inventory control, purchasing, and production. Others were clear savings in inventory holding costs, better purchasing costs, fewer people needed to control the part numbers, and so forth. Some products had increased materials costs as a result of these changes, but these additional costs were far outweighed by the broader savings accrued from the increase in commonality and reduction of variety within the process.

The same principles apply within the production processes. If the number of different processes can be reduced and more commonality of process introduced within the organization's product range, then the company will see enormous reductions in tangible and intangible costs. In addition, increased process commonality makes the company more flexible as customer product mix and product volume needs change.

Role of the Accountant in Variety Effectiveness

The analysis required to assess a company's variety effectiveness— both the positive and negative varieties—is a subtle task. There is a need to review the parts, products, and processes to determine all of these factors:

- Commonality
- Position of variability in the production process
- Variety benefits from the customer's perspective
- Financial impact of current variety

These analyses require the kind of analytic skills accountants have developed throughout their training.

Working with a team of engineers and production people, the accountants can bring a valuable perspective to the analysis. In particular, the accountants can develop methods for understanding the relative costs and benefits of different approaches. Very often, it is difficult to understand the cost impact of the current complexity and the benefits of undertaking the enormous task of eliminating unneeded variety. The accountants can assess the impact of the tangible and intangible costs. In addition, the analysis of the products, parts, and processes does not require engineering skills; instead, it requires skills in the type of statistical analysis that accountants use daily.

CONTINUOUS IMPROVEMENT

The objective of concurrent-engineering and cross-functional teams is to design the product "right the first time" so that it is perfect when first put into production: perfect quality, perfect production process, perfect features, and perfect cost.

We do not, however, live in a perfect world. While concurrent engineering has radically improved product design and reduced time to market, it is not uncommon for products to go into production without achieving their allowed cost. The processes of target costing and value engineering eliminate much of the excess cost, but often more improvement can be made.

Once the design project is complete, the processes of continuous improvement come into action. Target costs can continue to be set after the product is in production. Target-costing systems can have effective dates established so that cost improvements can continue to be worked on throughout the production processes. Value engineering teams can continue to extract costs from the product and the process. Even after the allowed cost is achieved, more improvement can be created.

Continuous improvement is a basic tenet of the total quality management (TQM) movement. Everybody in the company is responsible for improving quality and eliminating waste. Waste costs money. Eliminating waste reduces costs. The accountants need to be on quality improvement teams studying the products, production processes, and administrative processes, and continuously eliminating waste and improving quality. This is how accountants can become valuable, proactive professionals creating improvement and moving the company forward.

SUMMARY

The proliferation of new products and the need for fast time to market have led companies to adopt concurrent engineering methods of product design. Concurrent engineering requires a cross-functional team of professionals to work on product design from start to finish. Accountants have an important role to play on the concurrent-engineering teams.

In addition to serving as team members involved in every aspect of product design, accountants perform specific tasks requiring the use of new accounting techniques developed specifically for concurrent-engineering methods. These include:

- Target costing
- Value engineering
- Life-cycle costing
- Quality function deployment
- Variety-effectiveness analysis

These new approaches provide vital insight into the quest for products that have the following benefits:

- Products are enthusiastically accepted by the market
- Products have very high levels of quality

- Products can be made and distributed profitably
- Products reach the market quickly

In addition, the analytical skills of accountants can be used in many other aspects of the design process. This opens up exciting new avenues where accounting professionals can make a vital contribution to the company's success.

QUESTIONS

1. Why are progressive companies using new approaches to product design?
2. What is concurrent engineering? List some keys to success with concurrent engineering.
3. What are the definitions of *target profit, allowable cost,* and *target cost*? How could target-costing principles be best applied in your company?
4. What are three benefits of life-cycle costing? Is life-cycle costing applicable in your company? How would you begin to model life-cycle costs of new products:
   - By analogy
   - Heuristically
   - By calculation
   - Some other approach
5. How can house charts be used in your company to understand and focus on customer needs?
6. Does the accounting department have customers? How can the accounting department become more customer focused? Would a house chart be helpful in matching your department's "product" to the needs of the customer?

9

Implementing the New Approach to Accounting

There are two ways to approach the introduction of these new accounting methods: strategically or pragmatically. If the changes are introduced strategically, then they are driven from the top of the company and are a part of the organization's broader lean transformation. Senior management has caught the vision for a world-class organization and sees that the role of the accountants (and others) needs to change dramatically if the company is to succeed in its quest for world-class status. The changes are coordinated and companywide. A new role is defined for the accounting people (or by the accounting people), and these changes are introduced with education and training, the initiation of improvement events, the reorganization of the accounting department, and the integration of previously accounting functions into the operations departments. The strategic approach is fast, radical, and culture changing.

Unfortunately, it is common, particularly in larger companies, that the senior managers do not have the vision or organizational competence to make the kind of changes required to radically improve the business. It is common for executives of companies to state they are "going lean" and to issue all kinds of instructions to their divisions with regard to lean transformation, but without a real understanding of what they are asking for. It is a difficult enough job to change your thinking from a traditional company to a lean company when you are working in the plants and in the forefront of the changes. It is very difficult indeed for a corporate executive to really understand what is required to change a multinational corporation from the top down, for several reasons:

1. They got to the top of the company using traditional methods.
2. They are not involved in the detailed changes taking place in the business and therefore do not have a practical understanding of the impact of lean thinking.
3. Senior executives in public companies often have financial bonuses based on the achievement of short-term profitability and stock price, which leads them to take actions that are contrary to their expressed desire to transform the company.
4. Finally, the people at the top of large companies rarely hear the truth of what is happening within the company. The organization's command-and-control processes usually insulate executive management from real information pertaining to the company's operation.

If the changes cannot be effectively made from the top down, then implementing these new accounting methods must be approached from the bottom upward. The *bottom-up approach* to transforming accounting is more difficult to achieve, but very significant improvement can still be made within the organization by managers who seek the opportunity and understand the need for creative change. It is not necessary to have fundamental and strategic change taking place in the company for the local accounting people to reengineer their own roles and become more valuable members. They can gradually introduce changes within the organization, bring the financial systems into line with the needs of the operations, change their own role within the company, and re-create themselves from backward-looking number crunchers into forward-looking, proactive, valuable members of the organization.

MAKING THE CHANGES

Regardless of the origins of the changes taking place in the accounting community, the activities described in the following paragraphs are the starting points for creating a new, proactive role for accountants. Every company is different, and the specific approaches will be governed by the needs of the company, the needs of the market, and the level of lean transformation within manufacturing, product design, distribution, and sales and marketing. The following steps are a good structure to set about the task of transforming the accounting systems and the accountant's role. These changes are not easy to make, but they can be made easier if the people involved have actively chosen to change their ideas and their outlook.

Read Widely

It is common for most professional people within an organization to read magazines and books about the issues associated with their profession. Accountants read such magazines as *Journal of Accountancy* or *Strategic Finance,* and they read books dealing with new ideas on accounting topics. But this is not sufficient. If real change is to occur, it is necessary to begin to read and understand the issues associated with a wider range of disciplines.

It is well known that real change and improvement never come from the center of a discipline. Real changes, i.e., the paradigm shifts, are made by people on the periphery. Creative ideas rarely come from people who are the experts in a particular field, because they often cannot see the forest for the trees. Instead, creative change comes from people who are able to synthesize ideas from one aspect of business (or life in general) with ideas from another area. These ideas may not seem to naturally fit together; indeed, sometimes they actually appear to be in conflict. But this is the crucible of creativity in any walk of life.

Another similar approach is to attend meetings of trade associations aimed at other professionals, perhaps with people from your company who are working in very different fields from accounting. Take classes in nonaccounting subjects. Most larger companies have well-planned education and training programs for their employees, so take classes designed for production people, engineers, sales people, and so forth. If these classes are not available directly through your company, then seek them out at local colleges, universities, and adult education centers.

Read books that will broaden your scope of knowledge, particularly books that relate to nonaccounting aspects of your business. Make sure you understand the technology associated with the products your company makes. Make time to understand the production methods and philosophies employed in the company. Read books that are outside the realm of your company, books that will stimulate new ideas and new approaches.

Cultivate a Global View

Recognize that the world has changed radically and that every company is in a global market. Gain an understanding of the global issues affecting your company and your marketplace. Seek out information that will broaden your own understanding of the challenges your company is facing in the global marketplace. *The Economist* magazine is a good place to start.

Spend as much time as possible with the sales and marketing people of the company—not discussing variances or profitability, but discussing the issues they are facing day in and day out in the market. Delve deeply into such issues as these:

- The competitiveness of your company's products
- The value your company provides to the customer
- The gaps in the market
- New products in the making
- The changes in technology that are likely to affect your company's market position and competitiveness

Study your company's competitors. Become an expert in the competition's plans, strategies, and financial position. Get the information needed to understand what your competitors are doing and how their approaches differ from those of your own company.

Spend time with the design engineers and other people in the R&D (research and development) departments. Gain an understanding of the issues that are challenging your company. Investigate the historical development of the company's products, their attributes, why they were successful or failures, and what is being done to overcome limitations in the market. Examine the new technologies and ideas being developed by the R&D people, and understand how these new products will affect the marketplace.

Go to the shop floor and the warehouses more often. Understand the processes, understand those workers' views and approach, and become familiar with the issues they are facing. Perhaps volunteer to work a few shifts, perhaps the evening shift, so that you can become more intimately familiar with the shop-floor processes and procedures.

Create a Team

If you are finding a need within your company to take a radically different role, then it is likely that there are other people with similar feelings. Make a point of discussing these issues in a nonthreatening way with the people in your department and other related departments. If there is interest in pursuing these kinds of changes, then create a small team of enthusiastic volunteers. Work together to make these changes.

Some people start a small study group that meets once a week to discuss the issues. These study groups often include a reading circle where (outside of the group meeting) the people read a practical book on lean manufacturing, or cellular manufacturing, or lean accounting, or another important topic, and then come together to discuss the book and its relevance to their own situation.

It is easier to introduce these kinds of changes when you have a group of people working together than it is if an individual is working alone. Creating a group of like-minded company employees is a valuable step to creating change. Make sure the group remains positive. It is easy for a group of this sort to become focused on the company's shortcomings; every company has plenty of room for improvement. The best companies are the most self-critical. It is important that the group focuses on the need for change and the opportunities for change.

Learn about Lean Methods

Read the books and take the classes so that you become very familiar with the current trends in modern manufacturing. The accounting (and other) support people in a company are often criticized for being ignorant of the lean methods and principles the company is pursuing. This must be overcome. A starting point would be lean manufacturing methods. If there are no classes available,* use one of the many excellent books on lean† to gain an in-depth understanding of its processes and procedures. (See the References for some suggested titles.)

---

* www.ame.org and www.mep.nist.gov.
† *Lean Thinking* by James Womack and Daniel Jones, Free Press 2003; *Lean Production Simplified* by Pascal Dennis, Productivity Press 2007; *Learning to See* by Michael Rother and John Shook, Lean Enterprise Institite 1999; *Better Thinking, Better Results* by Robert Emiliani, CLBM 2007.

Learn about statistical process control (SPC). SPC is the foundation for the development of quality processes in industrial organizations. Most companies use SPC in production areas only; but SPC is applicable to a wide range of business situations (see Wheeler 1993). It is important that proactive accountants have a good understanding of the methods, strengths, and limitations of SPC.

Learn and use the seven management tools in the *Memory Jogger+* (see Brassard 1989; Mizuno 1979). These are methods that have been developed to apply the philosophies of quality control and problem solving in the broader context of management creativity and process improvement. Whereas classic TQM is concerned with gathering numerical data, analyzing it, and creating improvement from an understanding of statistics, the seven management tools in the *Memory Jogger+* are concerned with gathering and analyzing qualitative information about the business and using this to create improvement and radical change. These innovative methods of problem solving and team-based improvement are powerful tools for any agent of change.

Learn the concepts involved with production planning and control. If your company is currently endeavoring to use a manufacturing resource planning (MRPII) approach, then read the books about traditional MRPII methods (Arnold 1991; Vollmann and Whybark 1992). If the company is moving toward lean and world-class manufacturing methods, then study those issues and understand the concepts and the practicalities (Maskell 1994; Schonberger 1986). Many of these important new approaches are delayed or compromised because the accounting people do not have a clear understanding of the real goals of the changes, and they concentrate only on the accounting issues.

Process-Map Your Department's Activities

The best place to start putting these new methods into action is within your own department.* Don't just read the books and enjoy them; actively use the methods and gain a practical understanding of the techniques. The first reason for process mapping your own department is to gain an understanding of how to use the technique for process improvement. Try not to do this alone. These process mapping methods and the lean ideas are designed for team-based

---

* There is a detailed example on pages 12–16 of the book *The Lean Business Management System* by Brian Maskell et al., BMA Press, Cherry Hill, NJ, 2007.

improvement, and they work best when used by a small team. Try to create enthusiasm within your department for working together to understand the fundamental issues within your own areas and create improvement.

Once the process maps have been drawn, use the analytical tools to gain an understanding of the flow of work through the department. Determine value-added and non-value-added processes, assign primary and secondary classifications, and draw graphs of these measures. Look at the timeliness of the activities your department performs, understand the delays, and understand the quality problems and where they occur. Drill down deeply in the issues your department is facing. If necessary, bring in people from outside the area to provide a fresh look at the issues. Ask "why" five times and get to root causes of problems, even if the answers are uncomfortable.

Once the analysis has been done, it is usually quite straightforward to develop new processes and procedures that will overcome many of the problems, including non-value-added activities, quality problems, delays, and so forth. If there is no appetite for radical change within the department, it may not be possible to implement these changes fully, but that should not prevent the people in the department from developing the ideas and presenting them to the managers along with the backup analysis. Or you can employ the Jesuit school of management approach: since forgiveness is easier to obtain than permission, do it first and ask for permission later.

If you can make significant improvement in your own processes:

1. You will do some good and make your processes better.
2. You will begin to have a practical understanding of lean methods.
3. You will free up the time of the people in the accounting department so that time is available to work on further improvement.

Get Actively Involved in Lean Manufacturing

The only way to learn how lean manufacturing and lean thinking works is to actively do it. Accountants should be actively involved in working on the improvement teams within the factory, the design office, and the logistics processes, making improvement and eliminating waste. Most companies us the *kaizen blitz* approaches to lean change in the factory. These are typically five-day focused projects designed to analyze a production process and make significant changes. Accountants should volunteer to be members of these kaizen teams. People are busy and carving out five days to spend on something outside of your own work is hard to do. But this is essential if you are to understand lean and understand how the accounting systems can be changed to support the changes taking place within the company. In addition, the kaizen will be better for having an accountant on the team. Your perspective and skills will add a great deal to the improvement process.

Visit Other Companies

There are probably many excellent companies close to where you work. Make a habit of visiting customers and vendors. Initially, these visits may have to be arranged through the sales people or the purchasing people. They may want to be with you when you visit. But after a time, as these ideas become more widespread, it will be possible for you to visit the customers or the vendors and provide them with positive help or assistance, and you will learn from them at the same time.

When you read about companies in trade journals and other magazines, call the people mentioned in the magazine and discuss the issues that are raised in the article. If possible, arrange to make a visit. It does not have to be a long visit: one or two hours is sufficient. Most people are very willing to show off the good things they have achieved.

Speak to people at your trade association meetings. Find out about their companies. Visit the ones that are doing innovative and interesting things. Listen to what your counterparts at these companies are complaining about: they may reveal issues you need to look at and understand.

IMPLEMENTING THE ACCOUNTING CHANGES

The following approach is a proven method for introducing new accounting methods into an organization pursuing lean and world-class manufacturing. But every company is different, and you will need to adapt this to your own needs.

There are two issues that must be addressed before you get started. The first is the definition of the value-streams. To be able to make significant progress with new accounting methods, it is necessary to understand the company's value-streams. Most companies approach lean manufacturing by identifying the value-streams, drawing value-stream maps, and using kaizen events to make improvements. Sometimes these value-streams work well for lean accounting, but other times, you find that too many value-streams have been identified for effectively managing the business. Order-fulfillment value-streams are always defined in terms of the flow of materials through the production process. But we are looking for the value-streams that will be used to manage the business. Often it is necessary to group two or three value-streams together under a single value-stream manager to create an effective entity for the management of the business. Sometimes the first step in the process is to have a kaizen event with the senior management team of the company or the plant to determine how the value-streams will be set up from a management point of view.

The second issue is the approach to implementation. You can select one value-stream and introduce the new accounting approach in depth within that single value-stream. Once this "pilot" value-stream has been thoroughly implemented and the methods proven, you can roll the methods out across the rest of the organization. Another approach is to introduce the methods gradually into all of the value-streams simultaneously. There is no "right or wrong" answer to this question, but the team needs to decide which approach makes the best sense. The pilot approach is a cautious and safe way of introducing the new methods, but it means that there will be parallel accounting systems for some time. The parallel approach is more complicated but it means a minimum of redundant processing.

Step 1: Training in Lean Accounting

The purpose of the training is to get the team together and create a common understanding and shared objectives. These training classes are typically two or three days in length, and the outcome is a detailed plan for making these new accounting approaches a reality in your company.

Step 2: Kaizen Event Style Methods for Performance Measurements and Value-Stream Costing

The use of kaizen event style methods for introducing changes to the accounting systems has gained popularity. Most companies use kaizen events to introduce lean manufacturing, and similar approaches work well for the new accounting methods. The first kaizen event usually addresses performance measurements and value-stream costing.

During the three- or four-day kaizen, the team creates the performance measurements linkage charts and designs the measurement system for the company or plant, the value-streams, the production cells, and support departments. These measurements are then implemented in one or two locations, using visual boards. A detailed plan is also developed for the implementation of the performance measurement boards in each value-stream, cell, and department.

The kaizen also includes creating a detailed value-stream income statement for (typically) one value-stream. This requires the design of the "plain English" statement of decisions relating to the following issues:

- Gathering the value-stream financial information each week
- Changes to the chart of accounts
- How the new financial reports will be used to control costs, reduce costs, and improve profitability

When new performance measurements are introduced, it is important to eliminate all the old measurements. You should never add measurements; only replace them.

Step 3: Kaizen for Box Scores and Decision Making

This kaizen picks up from the previous kaizen with the development of the box scores. The box score requires value-stream capacity information to add to the value-stream performance measurements and financial information. Capacity analysis of the value-stream is completed during this kaizen, using information available on the value-stream maps. The box scores are then used to develop methods for making routine decisions like quoting, make/buy, profitability, capital acquisitions, etc. The box scores are also used to calculate the financial impact of the lean changes made in the value-streams.

After the kaizen, the traditional accounting and decision-making methods are eliminated and replaced by the box score and the decision-making methods developed during the kaizen.

Step 4: Kaizen for Transaction Elimination and Inventory Valuation

During this kaizen, the team examines the company's transactions with a view to how the number of transactions can be greatly reduced. Generally, the team does not actually eliminate any transactions during this kaizen;* instead, the team develops a "maturity path matrix" that shows what must be in place within the operation to enable transactions to be eliminated while maintaining excellent financial and operational control. The focus is usually on the transaction-heavy documents like shop-floor work orders, inventory tracking, purchase orders, and accounts payable processes.

Transactions are used in traditional systems to create a semblance of financial control when the processes themselves are out of control. The purpose of the maturity path matrix is to establish a clear understanding of what must be in place within the company's processes to eliminate the need for the transactions. In other words, what are the new controls within the processes that obsolete the transactions? This enables the team to determine in advance what changes are required and to build these improvements into the overall lean transformation plan.

This kaizen also addresses inventory valuation. There are three interrelated issues that must addressed:

1. Do we have low inventory?
2. Is the inventory under good visual control?
3. Do we need to track the inventory on the computer?

There are about seven different methods for evaluating inventory, and they need to be used according to the needs of the business. If the company has high inventory that is out of control,† and if it tracks the inventory on the computer, then it will be necessary to value the inventory with a traditional product cost for each item. As the inventory levels become lower and are brought under control through the use of visual systems, then much simpler valuation methods can be used. During this kaizen,

---

* Sometimes it is possible to eliminate the detailed labor reporting on the shop floor during the kaizen. In most companies, this wasteful practice is not needed and can be easily eliminated.
† Generally, inventory is considered "out of control" when supply exceeds 60–90 days, when many shortages disrupt production, or when there is a need for cycle counting to keep the inventory accurate.

the various methods of inventory valuation are examined, and the team decides which ones may be appropriate. The inventory for the value-stream is evaluated using each of the likely methods to gain an understanding of the methods and to decide which is the most appropriate.

If there is a need within the company to calculate individual costs for products or subassemblies, this will also be done during this kaizen.

Step 5: Full Implementation of Lean Accounting

After these initial kaizens have been completed and the new accounting methods have been in use for a long enough time to assess their validity and accuracy, then it is time to "switch off" the traditional system and use the simple value-stream costing information for managing the business, decision making, and financial reporting—both internal and external. Although this sounds like a single "flick the switch" moment, there can also be a maturity path with this approach. For example, some companies choose to continue tracking their inventories on the computer system, but switch off the labor and overhead rates. This means they continue to pursue inventory tracking and inventory value, but the costs shown are actual material costs only. The standard costs have gone away, but the inventory records are still in use. Later, they may decide to take the next step and eliminate the inventory tracking as their inventory comes under better control operationally.

Step 6: Sales, Operations, and Financial Planning

The introduction of sales, operations, and financial planning (SOFP) can be done at any stage in the implementation of these simpler accounting methods. The purpose of SOFP* is to create a single, formal, and effective planning process across the entire organization. The process results in an authorized "game plan" for the company each month, including all of the following:

- A sales plan
- Production plan

---

* For a more detailed explanation of SOFP, see Chapter 13 of *Practical Lean Accounting* by Brian Maskell and Bruce Baggaley, Productivity Press, New York, NY, 2004.

- Product introduction plan
- Continuous improvement plan
- Purchasing plan
- Financial forecasts that replace the budgeting process

SOFP is implemented using a fully cross-functional team including sales and marketing people, operations people, purchasing, new products, finance, and other key people in the organization. This team implements the SOFP method and then goes on to create the SOFP each month. The implementation process goes through the five primary steps of SOFP and works out in detail—for the pilot value-stream—how this step will work. The five steps are:

1. Demand planning
2. Capacity planning
3. SOFP planning meeting
4. Financial forecasting
5. Executive SOFP meeting

Although the SOFP process can be introduced in a short time, it does take several months of using the process before it becomes effective and useful within the organization. Patience is required because the process only occurs once a month, and it takes several cycles before the team is able to customize the process to meet the company's needs.

Step 7: Target Costing

Target costing is not generally introduced using kaizen events. The best way to approach this is with a practical, hands-on method. Select a new product at the earliest stage of its development. Conduct a training class in target-costing methods, and at the end of the training, work through in detail the first six steps of target costing:

1. Identify the customer
2. Match customer needs to product and service features
3. Measure customer satisfaction
4. Specify the customer need
5. Weight the customer needs

6. Calculate the value created for the customer

After this initial event, the team will repeat steps 1–6 in real life. The team will select customers and/or markets for the products and gather the information needed to truly understand the customers' needs and their satisfaction with the new product or the concepts presented. Using this quality function deployment approach, the team determines the value created for the customer by the product or products in question.

The next step is for the team to meet again for a two-day event and to go through steps 7–12 of the target-costing process. These steps include:

7. Identify value and features or characteristics
8. Target costs for product or service
9. Target costs for major components
10. Match value against cost throughout the value-stream
11. Match target cost to processes
12. Implement continuous improvement and value engineering to bring costs into line with targets

Once again, the team members work through the 12 steps, using their own knowledge and understanding. But after the event, the team will gather and analyze real information about the product, the market, and the processes so as create a cross-functional action plan to bring the value-stream costs into line with the value needs of the customers and the market.

After the team's first foray into target costing, the team members will again meet for another two-day event to create standardized work for target costing within the company. Although it is important to recognize that the methods of target costing will always be subject to continuous improvement, it is also important to establish a standardized approach to how target costing should be applied within your own organization. This standardized approach is then applied widely across the company for new products and for existing products.*

---

* It is a common misunderstanding to think that target costing applies only to new product design. Target costing is equally applicable to existing products and processes. (See *Practical Lean Accounting* by Brian Maskell and Bruce Baggaley, Productivity Press, New York, NY, 2004 and *Lean Business Management Sytem* by Brian Maskell and the BMA Team. BMA Press 2007.)

WHAT'S AN ACCOUNTANT TO DO?

The remainder of this chapter describes some other issues to think about when implementing new accounting processes.

Define Roles of the Accounting Department

It is important to understand the mission of your work if you are to be effective. If the goals and objectives of the accounting and finance group are not well defined and understood by the people in the department and throughout the company, then there is a need to develop and disseminate this definition. It takes a considerable amount of time and clear thinking to develop a definition of the role of the accounting department (or any other department). Time and clear thinking can often be scarce commodities. But it is important to create a jointly developed and understood philosophy for everything the department does.

Link this role definition to the strategic needs of the business and to the needs of the department customers. Remember that the accounting systems follow the needs of the operation, not the other way around! The "customers" of the finance and accounting department are mostly within the company, but they also include outside parties, such as the IRS, the SEC, company suppliers, and other partners. Make sure that the department's goals and objectives match the requirements of the customers and the company strategy. Once this is achieved, measure the time spent on the activities that are strategically important: this is the equivalent of value-added work in a department that is entirely non-value-adding.

Cross-Train

Provide cross-training within your own area. The more broadly based an accountant can be, the more useful and valuable he or she will be to the company. The starting point for cross-training is within the accounting group itself. Develop a plan for the people in the various accounting functions to cross-train each other and create a program for moving from one set of tasks to another within the department.

Make sure that everyone in the department understands that the purpose of doing this is to provide more flexibility and expertise within the department, and to be a starting point for a more profound cross-training when the accounting people will move outside the walls of their department. Recognize that some people will not want to participate. If this is a small number, then just allow them to stay outside the program. If it is a large number of people, then there is more work to be done with education and persuasion to convince these people of the necessity to move into a proactive role.

Apply Lean Thinking in Your Own Processes

Most accounting departments have six to eight primary processes. Make sure that these processes are subject to continuous improvement. There may be a need for large kaizen events to kick off these changes, but often these processes can be improved through the use of small and less dramatic continuous improvement projects. Either way, ongoing and continuous improvement of the processes is required. Do not fall into the trap of thinking that you can "lean out" your process in one event or project. The lean rule of thumb is that a process does not approach lean until it has had eight major redesigns using lean thinking. There is a lot of work to be done; there is a lot of waste to be eliminated. Make process improvement a part of your everyday work.

For example, one company in Mexico recognized a need for significant improvement of its accounting processes: AP, AR, payroll, month-end close, etc. But the accountants and staff, like most people, were already working hard every day and could not see how they would have time to do major improvement projects. So they set up a program they called "Wednesday morning improvement." The whole accounting department of eight people met every Wednesday morning for two hours. During these two hours, they worked on process improvement. They defined six major processes within their department and worked on each process for two months. They have a one-year calendar, and every two months, they moved onto another process. The team used a standard problem-solving method using an A3 visual method.*

During the first week, the team identified issues it wanted to solve. During the second week, the team mapped the process; during the third week, the team defined the "future state" map and the gap analysis. Over the succeeding weeks, they implemented practical changes to solve the problems; they measured the success of these changes; and finally, they standardized the changes.

This practical and disciplined approach led this accounting team to make very significant improvements in their processes and freed up a great deal of time for other tasks.

Eliminate Reports

Most companies produce too many reports, and many of these reports are often confusing and conflicting. Create a project to review the company's performance measurement methods. If it is possible, set up a team to do a full performance measurement development program (described in Chapter 7). If it is not possible to create so elaborate a project, at least develop the linkages between the company's strategic directions and the critical success factors (CSFs); then, assess the performance measurement approach in light of the strategically based CSFs.

Review the company's current measurement system against these critical issues, taking account of the nine criteria presented in Chapter 7. From this analysis, you will be able to significantly reduce the number and complexity of the reports used throughout the company, and you will be able to focus on reporting relevant and strategically important issues. Remember: we never *add* reports; we only *replace* reports. Cut the reports down to the minimum possible.

---

* The A3 approach has become popular recently. A3 is a single sheet of paper that is A3 in size (in the United States this would be 11" × 17") and shows the seven or eight steps of the standard problem-solving process. The improvement project is documented on this single sheet of paper, which is displayed on the team's measurement board. For more information about A3 see *Managing to Learn* by John Shook, Lean Enterprise Institute 2009.

Measure Your Department's Performance

Although many accounting and finance departments are very much involved in the performance measurement of the company, they often do not have methods of measuring their own performance. Remember that the accounting department provides a service to its "customers" inside and outside of the company. As a service department, it needs to understand its customers and their needs, and it needs to have methods of assessing how well these needs are met.

The basic measurements of quality, on-time delivery, cost, and customer service can be applied to the accounting department straightforwardly. Take the regular and repetitive aspects of the department's business and make quantitative measures of timeliness, errors, and effectiveness.

For a service department, it is usually most effective to measure quality in terms of customer satisfaction. This can be measured by constructing a simple survey of the people in the company (and outside the company) that use the accounting department; these will include

- Managers looking for information
- People submitting expense reports
- Vendors looking for payment

and so forth.

The survey needs to be short and easy so that it addresses the issues but is not burdensome to the customers. Address issues such as timeliness, completeness, relevance, as well as people issues, such as user friendliness, understanding of the business, willingness to help people outside your own responsibilities, and "going the second mile."

Introduce a 5S Program into Accounting

The idea of 5S (or industrial housekeeping) is to have a clearly defined and tidy workplace. The 5Ss refer to the Japanese words for these five concepts that lead to a planned and organized work environment:

1. Organization
2. Orderliness
3. Cleanliness

4. Standardized cleanup
5. Discipline

The 5S approach has been used primarily on the shop floor, where work areas are cleaned and tidied, the materials and tools are arranged conveniently, and only items required immediately are present. The thinking behind this is that:

- People work better and more effectively if their work spaces are well organized.
- Safety is enhanced when an area is orderly.
- Work is more efficient if the tools and materials required to do the job are readily available.
- Equipment is more long-lived if it is cleaned and cared for each day.

But the most important reason for 5S is to create a visual work environment where visual management methods can be used. Visual management is impossible if the work area—factory, office, or laboratory—looks like a teenager's bedroom!

There is no reason why this approach should be any less important in an office environment than a production area. There have been many highly successful introductions of 5S in administrative offices, product design departments, marketing areas, and accounting groups. Start by educating people on the ideas of 5S. Some people are offended by the suggestion that their work area is untidy, and other people do not see the significance of the approach; these people need to understand the reasons for making this change.

Move through the 5S program step by step. Introduce basic tidiness first, then move to "a place for everything and everything in its place," and finally move on to the full 5S approach. Use a measurement method so that offices can be assessed on their adherence to 5S. Create a planned and orderly environment.

Move Accountants into the Value-streams

Look at the practicality of moving the accounting functions into the company's value-stream. It is best to move the accounting functions both physically and in terms of reporting relationships; but if this is not possible politically, then move the people physically while retaining the original reporting structure. The benefit of this is that the accounting people can then be involved in the daily business of the company making products, shipping to customers, provisioning materials, tracking schedules, and so forth.

In most companies, the only problems encountered in making this move are political problems. Moving the cost and management accounting people into the area of the company they work on makes obvious sense and can be justified merely in terms of the time required to travel backward and forward. Moving the accounts payable people into the purchasing-and-receiving area can be more difficult to achieve, and moving the accounts receivable function into sales and marketing can also present some problems. But making these moves shows a real commitment to being involved and relevant.

Volunteer to Join Improvement Teams

An excellent way for an accountant to become more and more involved with the business is to get involved with improvement teams. In companies committed to lean change and continuous improvement, there are often kaizen teams that proliferate for improvement throughout the organization. It is easy to join these teams and make a contribution. In more traditional companies, it takes more effort to become involved in improvement activities because they often do not have a cross-functional approach, and they do not see a need to involve people who are not directly associated with the problem. The only way to get into these teams is to volunteer and make a contribution: become known as the helpful accountant.

The best place for accountants to get involved in improvement projects is within the operational areas of the business, such as:

- Order entry
- Customer service
- Materials control and planning
- Production
- Shipping and distribution
- New product development
- Marketing

Sales and operations planning is another project where the accountants can be very helpful. This is the establishment of a formal method for understanding the sales demand on the company, understanding the company's production capacity and capability, and matching these to the company's business strategy. The outcome of this monthly process is a medium-term production plan that has been agreed to by the sales and marketing people, the production operations people, the new product development people, and the senior management of the company. Most companies do this badly; join a team that will address these issues, and make the process very good.

There are, of course, hosts of other areas where an accountant can become involved, make a contribution, and learn something important about the company, its methods and procedures, and its people. Don't wait to be asked to join a team. Go out and volunteer—get involved.

Use Visual Systems in the Accounting Areas

The use of visual-systems concepts would help to make the accounting department accessible to other people within the company. A visual approach within the offices is simply using signs, diagrams, and messages to show people where to get information, where to find people, and where different things are located. Displaying people's pictures, their roles within the department, their phone numbers and e-mail addresses, and so forth, opens the department to people outside.

Posting information and performance measures on the walls of the department and around the company is very important so that people can see the results of their efforts. Display either company-wide performance or the performance of individual teams, projects, or value-streams. The presentation of information through graphics and diagrams helps to make the information understandable and useful to the people who need to use it. Designing forms and reports within the company for ease of use is another aspect of visual systems that is much neglected. Make a specific initiative to redesign the forms and reports to be easy to use.

SUMMARY

There is a vital and exciting new role for accountants in companies that are moving away from the traditional organization and embracing lean and world-class approaches to address the unpredictable marketplace of the twenty-first century. The accountant who sits isolated in his or her department, printing out historical reports, is becoming a relic of the past. Sadly, many of these people find that their companies no longer need that kind of work done, and when it is necessary, it can be done readily by well-designed computer systems. The accountant who can help his or her company to thrive is an accountant who can be an agent of change.

An agent of change embraces change as an opportunity, not a threat. An agent of change is willing to move into any area of the business and bring his or her analytical skills and unique perspective to bear on the solution to business problems. This requires a willingness to:

- Learn new tools and techniques
- Gain an understanding of a wide range of business issues
- Actively promulgate improvement

These changes are taking place in every company. In most companies, they are happening without any plan or recognition. In forward-looking companies, these changes are part of an overall plan to create a dynamic and lean team of empowered professionals ready to take on the best in the world and win. This is the future for the accountant in a world-class company.

Interlude

Accounting Is Boring, but Controllership Is Not

The observation above was made by Jerry Johnson of VF Corporation at a World-Class Management Accounting Conference in Arlington, Virginia. VF Corporation is one of the world's largest manufacturers of fashion apparel, and Mr. Johnson was, until his recent retirement, the vice president of finance and the chief financial officer. Mr. Johnson's presentation was entitled "Accounting Is Boring but Controllership Is Not," and it struck a chord with many of the accountants at the conference because Jerry presented some of the frustrations shared by all of us. And although he made these comments a long time ago—the conference was held in May 1991—they still ring true today.

Somewhere back in the 15th century, a fellow named Pacioli wrote the first text on double-entry bookkeeping. Very few people at the time knew it. Those few who did, moreover, didn't really care. And there are still those among us today who hold the view that his pioneering effort was the first and last development of any significance to have occurred in the entire history of the subject. And I'm one of them. It seems to me that an awful lot of what has happened to accounting during the intervening five centuries— and most particularly in the past 15 years—has a lot to do with dividing up assets between creditors and owners (which was Pacioli's original purpose) and very little to do with running a business successfully.

In the past 30 years, the continuing refinement of functional organizational structures linked increasingly and exclusively only by a common management accounting system has gradually stripped companies of their natural ability to adapt to change. And so, when external change presents itself for consideration, it is roundly dismissed.

My question to you management accountants is this: "After this conference, what are you going to do differently on Monday morning?" Or are you comfortable with the notion that real-world problems are going to be solved by the implementation of a new management accounting system? Or that you really believe a change in systems will lead to a change in outcomes?

Of course, we're kidding here ... aren't we?

One of the lessons of accounting history is that most system changes—even those thought to foreshadow monumental improvement—produced major consequences unintended by their sponsors and many created more problems than they solved.

Please don't misunderstand me. I am not against modernizing our systems. We have been pursuing new accounting methods at VF for two years, and I'm very pleased with the results so far. And we are beginning to step off in the direction of non-financial performance measures. But let us not lose sight of the most important ingredient in the recipe for major change—YOU.

It sounds like I am beginning to say that just-in-time (lean manufacturing) should begin in the controller's department—and I am. Because I honestly believe that one of the most powerful forces resisting change in most organizations is the controller. Most controllers are busy, careful about their work, diligent in supervising their subordinates, thorough in reviewing the numbers, cautious in voicing their unqualified support for any project, extremely critical in voicing their reservations, encyclopedic in their knowledge of the historical events, and generally pretty miserable people to be with.

My message is that it does not have to be that way. Despite the odds, it really doesn't have to. But the difference between where you are and where you want to be is up here. It's in your mind, it's in your attitude. If you and I are going to make an impact in our companies—and I firmly believe we can—then each of us is going to have to get personally involved and begin to assume some personal responsibility for change.

The opportunity you have when you get back to your companies is to get personally involved inside the network of good ideas. Your mission is to find it, join it, and help it to grow. It's as simple as that. No script, no procedures manual, and no really solid guidelines. If you really want to play a leadership role in bringing about constructive change, you can—and you will probably have a good time doing it as well. The role of the controller is so different today than it was a few years ago, and many of us have been caught unawares. Old virtues have been superseded by new requirements:

- Knowledge must become curiosity
- Experience must become thoughtfulness
- Diligence must become dedication

- Thoroughness must become open-mindedness
- Conservatism must become enthusiasm
- Accuracy must become relevance

All that remains is *integrity*, which is a sufficient end in itself.

Interlude

Bean Counters No More

"Bean Counters No More"* was the theme of an issue of *Management Accounting* magazine, the journal of the Institute of Management Accountants in Montvale, New Jersey. Although this issue appeared many years ago, its ideas still resonate today. Most of the magazine was dedicated to case studies of companies in which the accounting people had shed the old image of the "green eyeshade" accountant laboring in a back room to produce irrelevant, incomprehensible, and late reports. These accountants had made the transition to "agents of change."

Technical Editor Susan Jayson noted:

> The number one complaint of management accountants with ten years or more experience is that "management doesn't listen to us. We have a lot of knowledge about the company, but when it comes to key business decisions, we are not in the loop. We are thought of as bean counters. Given the chance, we could really add value."

SOUTH CENTRAL BELL

Steven Harrison, manager of regulatory accounting at South Central Bell, said,

> We were able to shed our scorekeeper image forever by showing how accountants can be value-added business partners and an integral part of the management team. To do this, we had to step out of the traditional role of compilers, and take on the roles of interpreter, advisor, and partner.

---

* Extracts used by permission of the Institute of Management Accountants, Montvale, New Jersey.

In his article "Not Just Bean Counters," Mr. Harrison went on to relate the story of how deregulation in the telephone industry threw South Central Bell into a reporting nightmare. The old reporting systems were disbanded with the demise of "Ma Bell," and there was no agreement among the managers of the new company. There was a sharp and partisan conflict. It was decided that the accountants should take a proactive role.

During the next year, employees from the comptroller's department attended staff meetings with employees from the marketing and network departments. At some meetings, they gave presentations. At other sessions, they just listened—but they were present. Thus, the accountants learned about the concerns of the marketing manager and saw the difficulties caused by some of their existing policies and procedures.

They spent weeks with the marketing and network employees examining in great detail the cost-allocation process. This exchange gave marketing and network employees a much better understanding of the accounting processes, and it gave the accountants a much more complete understanding of the field operations and a chance to see parts of the business they normally did not run into.

In one state, a comptroller department employee was transferred to the network department to lend financial expertise. In another state, a comptroller department person was moved into the marketing department. In yet another state, at the annual marketing awards banquet, a member of the comptroller's department was awarded a "Spirit of Service" award to recognize his contribution. He was the first accountant to be awarded this prize.

AUTOMATIC FEED COMPANY

Nathan Weaks, treasurer of Automatic Feed Company, shared his viewpoint:

> The key is convincing managers we can solve more problems than we create! Unfortunately, accountants tend to get absorbed in financial reporting. They are more concerned with meeting the needs of outsiders. Consequently, the accountant's inside customers, who are critical to his or her advancement, get little direct benefit.

Automatic Feed Company was facing enormous problems with scheduling production. This came to a head when its largest customer threatened to cancel the company's largest-ever order if Automatic Feed Company did not start delivering on time. This crisis gave rise to an opportunity for the company's newly appointed treasurer to show that an accountant can be an agent of change.

To the astonishment and amazement of his colleagues in operations, marketing, and engineering, the treasurer quickly analyzed the situation and was able to develop an innovative and challenging solution to this chronic and damaging problem. The solution was not an easy one; it broke the paradigms and trod on a few toes. And many people were taken aback when the president assigned the treasurer to head up the team that was to implement the new scheduling system.

Using a four-step, team-based approach, Mr. Weaks studied the problem in detail, defined the new approach, applied simplifying procedures, piloted the methodology, and implemented the new system in about six months. The new approach was simple, proven, low cost (less than $10,000 of software development), and very effective.

The company's ability to keep promises and deliver on time was a major contributing factor to the doubling of annual sales, and the new scheduling system has been an important tool for identifying bottlenecks to company growth. In addition, when large projects are involved, the output reports from the scheduling system are automatically sent to customers because they have proven to be valuable customer communication tools.

Mr. Weaks concluded:

> Traditionally in Automatic Feed's engineering-manufacturing environment, the accounting function has been a second-class citizen. But solving the scheduling problem has changed that mentality. Scheduling has enabled our accountants to become more knowledgeable about our products— especially the products of design and manufacture. As managers came to trust and use the information provided by the scheduling system, the accountants have become accepted members of the management team.

Appendix

Accounting and Measurement Questionnaire

The purpose of this questionnaire is to help the company assess where the current accounting and measurement methods stand in relation to the company's needs, and where the company needs to be in the foreseeable future. Here are the categories and subcategories:

- Performance measurement
  Alignment of company strategy and lean goals
  Performance measures
  Empowerment and learning
- Value-stream costing
  Value-stream organization
  Product costing
- Measuring financial benefits
  Continuous improvement
  Financial benefits of lean changes
- Managing value-stream profitability
  Decision making
  Customer value and target costing
- Eliminating transactions
  Accounts payable and procurement
  Accounts receivable
  Authorizations and sign-offs
  Month-end figures
  Material costs
  Labor and overhead costs

Inventory tracking
• Value-stream management
Rewards and recognition
Role of finance people
Budgeting and planning

Each subcategory has four brief descriptions:

1. *Traditional*: A company that has traditional accounting and measurement methods
2. *Developing a framework*: A company that is making a start with lean
3. *Managing by value-stream*: A company with a progressive lean approach
4. *Lean business management*: A company with an advanced lean organization

These descriptions will not be 100% applicable to every company. They are intended as a guide to help you think out your accounting and measurement approaches in a logical and business-focused way.

INSTRUCTIONS

1. Read all four statements carefully:
   • 1. *Traditional*: The left-hand statement defines 1–2 on the scale.
   • 2. *Developing a framework*: The second statement covers the 3–4 range on the scale.
   • 3. *Managing by value-stream*: The third statement covers 5–6 on the scale.
   • 4. *Lean business management*: The right-hand statement defines 7–8 on the scale.
   (Please note: the statements and the numerical ratings do not precisely align. Some judgment is needed.)
2. Honestly evaluate the present position of your organization in terms of the four statements by marking an X (one of 1, 2, 3, 4, 5, 6, 7, 8) over the number that best represents your present position.

3. Decide where you would like your organization realistically to be in the foreseeable future by marking an O on the scale (one of 1, 2, 3, 4, 5, 6, 7, 8). This goal should be challenging yet realistic.

Here is an example:

Questionnaire Results Summary		*CURRENT*	*FUTURE*
Performance Measurement	Alignment of Company Strategy and Lean Goals		
	Performance Measures		
	Empowerment and Learning		
Value Stream Costing	Value Stream Organization		
	Product Costing		
Measuring Financial Benefits	Continuous Improvement		
	Financial Benefits of Lean Changes		
Managing Value Stream Profitability	Decision Making		
	Customer Value and Target Costing		
Eliminating Transactions	Accounts Payable & Procurement		
	Accounts Receivable		
	Authorizations and Sign offs		
	Month End		
	Material Costs		
	Labor and Overhead Costs		
	Inventory Tracking		
Value Stream Management	Rewards and Recognition		
	Role of Finance People		
	Budgeting and Planning		
	Average	0.00	0.00

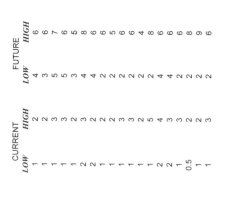

| Jackson A | | Jackson B | | Jackson C | | Visitors | | CURRENT | | FUTURE | |
CURRENT	FUTURE	CURRENT	FUTURE	CURRENT	FUTURE	CURRENT	FUTURE	LOW	HIGH	LOW	HIGH
2	5	2	4	2	6	1	5	1	2	4	6
2	4	1	3	2	6	1	4	1	2	3	6
3	5	3	5	2	7	1	5	1	3	5	7
2	5	3	5	3	6	1	5	1	3	5	6
2	4	2	3	1	5	1	4	2	2	3	5
2	4	3	4	3	8	2	4	2	3	4	8
1	2	2	3	2	6	2	4.5	1	2	2	6
1	2	2	3	2	5	2	3	1	2	2	5
2	4	1	3	2	6	3	4	1	3	2	6
2	3	3	4	2	4	1	2	1	2	2	4
4	5	1	3	5	8	1	4	1	5	2	8
3	5	4	5	2	6	2	4	2	4	4	6
1	2	2	6	3	6	2	3	2	3	4	6
1	2	1	4	2	8	0.5	5	0.5	2	2	8
1	3	1	2	2	9	1	3	1	2	2	9
2	3	2	3	3	6	1	2	1	3	2	6

References

Ansari, Shahid. 1999. *Target Costing*. Burr Ridge, IL: Richard D. Irwin Publishing.

Arnold, J. R. 1991. *Introduction to materials management*. Englewood Cliffs, NJ: Prentice Hall.

Brassard, Michael. 1989. *Memory jogger plus+*. Methuen, MA: GOAL/QPC.

Church, Alexander Hamilton. 1908. *The proper distribution of expense burden*. New York: John R. Dunlap.

Church, Alexander Hamilton. 1919. *Production factors in cost accounting and works management*. London: Engineering Magazine Press.

Cooper, Robin. 1995. *When lean enterprises collide*. Cambridge, MA: Harvard Business School Press.

Cooper, Robin, and Regine Slagmulder. 1997. *Target costing and value engineering*. New York: Productivity Press.

Cunningham, Jean, and Orest Fiume. 2004. *Real numbers: Management accounting in a lean organization*. Durham, NC: Managing Time Press.

Dennis, Pascal. 2006. *Getting the right things done*. Cambridge, MA: Lean Enterprise Institute.

Dennis, Pascal. 2007. *Lean production simplified*. New York: Productivity Press.

Dixon, John V. 1992. Focusing customer service on profits. Unpublished article. Middle Tennessee State University.

Fishman, Charles. 2006. No satisfaction at Toyota. *Fast Company* 111 (December). http://www.fastcompany.com/magazine/111/open_no-satisfaction.html?page=0%2C0.

Goldman, S. L., R. N. Nagel, and K. Preiss. 1994. *Agile competitors and virtual organizations*. New York: Van Nostrand Reinhold.

Hartley, John R. 1992. *Concurrent engineering*. Portland, OR: Productivity Press.

Hiromoto, Toshiro. 1988. Another hidden edge: Japanese management accounting. *Harvard Business Review* 66 (4): 22–26.

Ishikawa, Kaoru. 1982. *Guide to quality*. White Plains, NY: Asian Productivity Organization.

Johnson, H. Thomas. 1992. *Relevance regained*. New York: The Free Press.

Jones, Daniel, and James Womack. 1996. *Lean thinking*. New York: Simon and Schuster.

Kaplan, Robert S., and Steven R. Anderson. 2004. Time driven activity-based costing, *Harvard Business Review* 84, no. 11: 131.

Kaplan, Robert, and Thomas Johnson. 1987. *Relevance lost: The rise and fall of management accounting*. Cambridge, MA: Harvard Business School Press.

Mann, David. 2005. *Creating a lean culture*. New York: Productivity Press.

Maskell, Brian. 1994. *Software and the agile manufacturer*. Portland, OR: Productivity Press.

Maskell, Brian, and Bruce Baggaley. 2004. *Practical lean accounting*. New York: Productivity Press.

Maskell, Brian, Bruce Baggaley, Nick Katko, and David Paino. 2007. *The lean business management system*. Cherry Hill, NJ: BMA Press.

Mizuno, Shigeru. 1979. *Management for quality improvement: The 7 new QC tools*. Cambridge, MA: Productivity Press.

Monden, Yasuhiro. 1992. *Cost management in the new manufacturing age*. Portland, OR: Productivity Press.

Peters, Tom. 1994. *The Tom Peters seminar*. New York: Random House.

Pine, Joseph. 1993. *Mass customization*. Boston: Harvard Business School Press.

Rother, Michael, and John Shook. 1999. *Learning to see*. Cambridge, MA: Lean Enterprise Institute.

Sakurai, Mishiharu. 1992. Target costing and how to use it. In *Emerging practices in cost management*, ed. Barry J. Brinker. Boston: Warren, Gorham & Lamont.

Schonberger, Richard. 1986. *World class manufacturing*. New York: The Free Press.

Seddon, John. 2005. *Freedom from command and control: Rethinking management in lean service*. New York: Productivity Press.

Shook, John and Chet Marchwinski. 2003. *The Lean Lexicon*. Brookline, MA: Lean Enterprise Institute.

Solomon, Jerold. 2004. *Who's counting: A lean accounting business novel*. New Haven, IN: WCM Associates.

Stocker, Gregg. 1992. Quality function deployment: Listening to the voice of the customer. In *APICS 35th International Conference Proceedings*, Montreal.

Surowiecki, James. 2008. Toyota: The open secret of success. *New Yorker*, May 5.

Vollman, Berry, and D. Clay Whybark. 1992. *Manufacturing planning and control systems*. New York: Business One Irwin.

Wheeler, Donald J. 1993. *Understanding variation*. Knoxville, TN: SPC Press.

White, R. E. 1993. Empirical assessment of JIT in U.S. manufacturers. *Production and Inventory Management Journal* 34 (2): 38–42.

About the Author

Brian H. Maskell, president of BMA Inc., has more than 30 years of experience in the manufacturing and distribution industry. He has held a variety of management positions, from the shop floor of an electronics company to manager of European inventories for the Xerox Corporation to vice president of product development and customer service of the Unitronix Corporation. Over the past 15 years, Mr. Maskell has been a consultant for many manufacturing and distribution companies in the United States, England, Mexico, Australia, South Africa, Europe, and the Far East. He has assisted these companies in the implementation of advanced manufacturing techniques, including lean and agile manufacturing, logistics and supply-chain management, lean accounting, value-stream costing and management, new performance measurement, process reengineering, enterprise information systems, and total quality management.

A sought-after speaker, Brian Maskell is the author of several books, including:

The Lean Business Management System (2007)
Life's Little Lean Accounting Instruction Book (2006)
Practical Lean Accounting (2003)
Performance Measurement for World Class Manufacturing (1991)

He has also created a video presentation entitled "Lean Accounting" (2004), available from the Society of Manufacturing Engineers. Mr. Maskell's works address the needs of manufacturers in the increasingly competitive twenty-first century. Mr. Maskell conducts seminars and workshops around the world on such subjects as lean accounting, lean business management, performance measurement for world-class manufacturing, lean manufacturing, value-stream cost management, target costing, and agile manufacturing.

Mr. Maskell has an engineering degree from the University of Sussex, England. He is certified with the Chartered Institute of Management Accountants (CIMA) in London, the American Institute of Certified Public Accountants (AICPA), the Institute of Management Accountants (IMA), and he is a Fellow of the American Production and Inventory

Control Society (APICS). He is the author of numerous articles and papers and regularly presents papers at national and international conferences, and he teaches occasionally at Wharton Business School.

He can be contacted at:

E-mail:	bmaskell@maskell.com
Tel:	609 239 1080
Web:	www.maskell.com
	www.BMAEurope.com

Index